D1453902

THE ULTIMATE SOUP BOOK

THE ULTIMATE SOUP BOOK

Mary and Mike Spencer

CELESTIAL ARTS
Millbrae, California

First Printing, September 1975

Made in the United States of America

Celestial Arts

231 Adrian Road

Millbrae, California 94030

Library of Congress Cataloging in Publication Data

Spencer, Mike, 1937-
    The ultimate soup book.
    Includes index.
    1. Soups. I. Spencer, Mary, 1943- joint author.
II. Title.
TX757.S64   641.8'13   75-9085
ISBN 0-89087-057-8

CONTENTS

To our 11-year-old son, Sean, whose quaint "yuk!" failed to discourage our research or dampen our enthusiasm for some of the more exotic entries in this book. May his troubles never exceed those presented by a cold avocado or Virginia peanut soup.

FOREWORD

A psychologist of our acquaintance warns people to "beware of experts" because, he says, after a while they start believing their own nonsense and become dangerous. That pretty well sums up our feelings about the "experts" in the culinary arts; those who insist that you must *never* do certain things while you must *always* do others. As is the case with most extremists, they deal strictly in terms of black or white, right or wrong. Only they are blessed with The Word or in this case The Taste.

Bosh!

You are the expert. It is your taste which determines what is right and what is wrong in cooking. It doesn't make much sense to us, for example, to eat something laced with garlic when you don't like garlic— even if Julia Child does. We recognize, of course, that there are certain basic rules which must be followed in cooking (don't serve pork rare, don't eat spaghetti or rice uncooked, etc.), but we assume anyone who can spread butter already knows them. If they don't know the basics, they won't be in the kitchen anyway and they certainly wouldn't be buying this or any other cookbook.

We especially dislike this pretentiousness in restaurants, so much so that we routinely boycott those which try to shove their tastes down our throats. We know one restaurateur of high reputation, for example, who considers sweet salad dressings some form of heresy and serves only a yogurt dressing at his famed establishment. Well, we don't particularly care for yogurt on salads and, frankly, sometimes (this should be said almost as an apology, of course) we prefer a light, sweet dressing—maybe honey-lemon or creamy avocado. What we really resent, though, are the raised brows when we suggest such sacrilige to the Great Man or one of his equally pompous waiters. We don't go back.

We personally don't care for well-done steaks and, in all candor, have great difficulty understanding how anyone can like them burned. After all, the flavor is gone, the tenderness is gone, the juiciness gone. But, we have a friend who, like millions of other people across the land, likes his meat done just that way. His problem, of course, is that he cannot get it in most restaurants. Most have notations like this on the menu: "We Do Not Serve Steaks Well Done." We even found one restaurant where the notation reads: "Our Chef Prepares Steaks Rare Only." Our feeling is that the chef can also eat them—all. We believe our friend and his millions of counterparts have a perfect right to be wrong and eat their meat any way they order it. Maybe you can't be choosy at the Midnight Mission, but you certainly can in a restaurant when the money's coming out of your pocket.

You may well be wondering at this point what all of this has to do with soups. Well, in a roundabout way, a great deal. What we are attempting to do here is to puncture some of the pomposity which reigns over the preparation of fine meals; to shatter if we can some of the mystique. We are convinced you don't need a certificate from the Cordon Bleu in Paris to be able to delight your own and friends' palates. Au contraire, monsieurs et mesdames, we are firmly convinced that cooking is—now get ready for this one—EASY and fun. It's a game any number can play—and enjoy.

We can't help but wonder sometimes if maybe the make-it-look-hard school hasn't played a major role in the steady deterioration of the American diet. "Convenience" foods rule the marketplace and once Madison Avenue has you convinced that they are indeed convenient, what does that make the other foods? Inconvenient, of course. Time consuming in preparation. Difficult. Bothersome. As a result, few people make anything from scratch anymore; few feel they have the time. After all, you can conveniently find anything you want or need on the supermarket shelves or in their freezer compartments. Not only do most people not make things themselves, they are astounded that you do. A quick example: We make our own peanut butter and any number of times we have had people ask in amazement how we do it. They are even more amazed when we tell them that all we do is throw some peanuts into the blender and add a little butter for consistency.

Like Pavlov's dog, our taste buds have been conditioned to not only accept imitation or adulterated foods, but to actually prefer them. Official government statistics show people in America today eat less fresh fruits and vegetables than at any time in history; that they prefer dead white bread to the incredibly nourishing stone-ground wheat variety; that they prefer artificially flavored strawberry ice cream to the genuine item. As a case in point, several years ago we joined another family for a day-long outing at the beach and volunteered to bring the dessert. We toted along our hand-crank ice cream maker and all the ingredients—raw milk, raw cream, honey and fresh peaches off a neighbor's tree. The kids enjoyed making the ice cream, but only our son—who is accustomed to homemade foods—enjoyed eating it. The others complained it was "too sweet." What they meant, of course, was that it was too rich. They had never in their lives eaten *real* ice cream.

We mourn the passing of real ice cream and real mayonnaise and real peanut butter and tree-ripened fruits and vine-ripened vegetables, but most of all, we mourn the disappearance of the stockpot from the family kitchen. America has been "Campbellized" and, again, restaurants must take a good deal of the blame for this sad situation because for the most part have done nothing to head it off. Instead, they have thrown in the dish towel. The can-opener has replaced the stock pots there, too, and instead of fresh soups we are treated to something that resembles watered down bean puree during the week and canned clam chowder on Friday. Their attitude, to paraphrase the endearingly witty Marie Antoinette, seems to be : "Let them eat Campbell's!" Well, it need not be so.

Soups sweep the culinary gamut. They can be subtle or grand, budget meals or lavish feasts; they can provide a gentle introduction to a meal or they can dominate it. They can even cap it off as a dessert. In the simplest form, as what was called Hobo Soup, soup is incredibly cheap (hobos would, and maybe still do, stop by a cafe and order a cup of tea, drink it and ask for a refill of hot water. Then, they would add sugar, lots of ketchup, cream, salt and pepper and—voila!—tomato soup). At the other end of the spectrum is the crab bisque we innocently threw together for a New Year's Eve party late-night snack. The cost not only boggled our budget but our minds as well, even though the "snack" was an absolute triumph as far as the guests were concerned.

While you will not find the complete recipe for Hobo Soup in this book (the brief description above will simply have to suffice for those interested), you will find the bisque. And, in keeping with our insistence that your taste is the only one that really counts, we have included a number of soups we did not personally find appealing. For awhile we seriously considered including them all in a separate chapter entitled something like *We Didn't Like These, But You Might*, but discarded that notion in favor of slipping them into the areas where they belonged by origin, ingredients, or what have you.

We have also done something not all of our cookbook author colleagues do (a little trade secret unmasked!) and that is we have brewed and tasted every recipe in this book.

We have only one little hint to leave you with before you enter the world of soups: Never be afraid to use more of any of the basic ingredients than the recipe calls for—as long as it's something for which you have a special fondness. Never be afraid to experiment. All recipes are merely guides or outlines. You fill in the blanks and that's why we've included room for notes or comments. It's an idea we stole from Mike's grandmother's personal cookbook. She would write in the recipes before trying any of them, then after giving them a go, would make notations such as: "Tastes better with two instead of three tablespoons of orange juice" or "Clarify butter first" or "Forget it!!!"

We are hopeful that any entries you make will be more positive than Grandmother's one-word final judgment and are confident that they will be—if your tastes are anything like ours.

one

ESSENTIAL TOOLS

As is the case with any endeavor, there are some basic tools of the trade—the essentials, without which soups are impossible.

- A stockpot, of course, tops the list because without stock there is no soup. We suggest the two-gallon stainless steel variety. Actually, we suggest two of them so that you can have two stocks going at the same time.
- A blender is another essential. You don't need the kind that blends, dices, heats, liquefies, chops, chips and even putts if you want it to. The cheapest two or three-speed variety will do just fine.
- A large slotted spoon is important for skimming off the top of stock as it cooks and cools.
- Freezer jars come in handy for storing leftover stock, but old mayonnaise jars do just as well.
- Cheesecloth (or a large stainless steel tea caddy) is needed for bouquet garni. Essential ingredients in the garni (further explained in the section on basic stocks) are bay leaf, thyme, celery leaves and fresh parsley.

two

STOCKS AND OTHER BASICS

We have a friend who was born and reared in a tiny town in the Deep South. From his earliest years he loved to sketch and paint and by the time he reached his mid-teens had earned quite a local reputation for his artistic talents. Of course, his world only stretched about five miles in any direction and encompassed a mere 500 people, but in it he was Picasso. When he reached 17, he decided to share his genius and, after carefully piecing together a portfolio of his better works and scraping up a few dollars, struck out for a foreign land known as Shee-Cago. Several days of riding rails, hitchhiking and walking found him in the fabled city and he was able to land an appointment with the art director of the Tribune. With the confidence known only to fools or those who have genius and recognize it, he arrived late for his appointment (not wanting to appear anxious, you see) and sat back awaiting the accolades he knew were coming. The art director carefully went through each drawing, then neatly placed them all in order and handed them back.

"I like the way you sign your name," he said. "Come back when you learn to draw."

Our friend, who today is quite successful as an art director himself, realizes now that he lacked some basics. He had the ingredients—pencils, brushes, paper, a natural talent, desire and

7

an eye for colors—but he did not know how to put them all together.

The same is certainly true of soups. You can have the highest quality ingredients and still come up with slightly flavored water. The secret lies in the stock. And the secret of the stock lies in the bouquet garni. For want of a bouquet garni, the stock is lost. For want of a stock, the soup is lost.

So, before we get into the actual stocks and their preparation, let's get the bouquet garni out of the way. It is a simple mixture of parsley, celery leaves, bay leaves and thyme. The recipe:

1 bay leaf
4 sprigs parsley
leaves from 1 stalk celery
2 sprigs fresh thyme (or ½ teaspoon dry thyme)

If you are using fresh items—and we are great believers in fresh-fresh-fresh—you can simply tie the ingredients together with string. If you are using dry ingredients, place them in a piece of cheesecloth and tie the top. Or, place them in a large stainless steel tea caddy.

The garni provides essential flavoring and is dropped into the stockpot along with other ingredients first thing and left in until the stock is done.

We thought we had lost either the golden touch or our minds one evening while putting the finishing touches to a poultry stock. It had simmered and brewed and steeped for hours; it contained a full five-pound chicken and everything else required for a delectable dish—but it had almost no taste. We cursed the chicken. We cursed the butcher who quartered and sold the beast to us. We cursed the moon. Then we realized we had left out the garni, popped it in, simmered the stock a few more hours—and, voila!, regained the magic touch.

Vegetables form one of the important bases for any stock and when we first got into soups we were mystified as to why most recipes called for straining out the vegetables after the simmering process was completed. Why strain out the vegetables? It didn't make any sense to us, so we ignored that instruction. Instead, we would liquefy the vegetables in the blender after stir-frying them and then swirl the mixture into the other ingredients in the stockpot. That way we could have our vegetables and eat them too. The question itself, however, went unanswered, but not forgotten. Some years later, we were talking with Perla Meyers, the marvelous culinary magician who operates the International Kitchen in New York City and who authored *The Seasonal Kitchen, a Return to Fresh Foods.* Incidentally, Perla's recipe for avocado soup is the best we have ever tested and it's included in this book—properly credited, of course. During the conversation, soups and our plans for this book came up and back came the question. Why strain vegetables from the stock? Perla said she didn't know either, but would check it out. Her answer came back in a couple of weeks. It seems, says Ms. Meyers, that most of the recipes were originated before the invention of the blender and were passed down in families and books in the original form. Vegetables were strained to keep the stock from turning out lumpy.

Now to the stocks themselves. As we said, for want of a stock, the soup is lost and nothing could be more true. Properly done, however, few things are easier than brewing a rich, thick, aromatic, tasty and nutritious stock. One of the beauties of the stock process is that just about anything goes—into it, that is. Slap the hands of the box boy who starts to tear off the carrot tops—they go into the pot, as do potato peels, carrot peels, mushroom stems, pea pods, celery base, any vegetable, scrap of meat or bone. The base itself can be leftovers. With poultry stock, for instance, a turkey carcass is the perfect starting point. Another beauty of stock is that it isn't exclusively for soups; it's also a marvelous base for gravies and meat sauces.

In the section on Essential Tools, we mention freezer jars or old mayonnaise jars. The reason is simple. The recipes listed here make upwards of three quarts of stock and it's seldom you will be using an entire batch for one sitting or one soup. So, freeze it and when you're in the mood for a little soup, three-quarters of the work is done once the stock is thawed. We use mayonnaise jars and our freezer always has at least six or seven containers marked "beef" or "chicken" or "fish."

One tip and one reminder before we detail the half-dozen stocks which act as the keys to the world of soups. With the exception of poultry or fish, any bones used in stocks should be broken or severely cracked to allow the marrow to seep into and blend with the liquid. Cooking a whole bone is about as valuable as cooking a whole rock. And, don't forget the bouquet garni.

BEEF STOCK

4 quarts water
2 pounds beef (shank or brisket), cut into pieces
4 pounds cracked beef bones
2 carrots, diced
2 onions, diced
2 celery stalks, diced (include tops)
2 garlic cloves
2 tablespoons butter
1 tablespoon vegetable oil
1 tablespoon tomato paste
2 teaspoons salt
bouquet garni

Saute vegetables (reserving celery and garlic) in the butter and oil until onion is clear. Liquefy in blender, adding a little of the water. Mix into water. Roast the bones for about 30 minutes in baking dish (the meat can be browned along with the bones or browned in a heavy skillet). Place all the ingredients in stockpot and bring to boil. Reduce to simmer, partially cover and cook for about 4 hours, continually removing any scum and fat that comes to surface. Remove bones and celery and allow stock to completely cool, again removing any fat or scum that surfaces. Refrigerate or freeze in individual containers. As with the chicken stock, you can simply pop the whole stockpot into the refrigerator, but make sure you take it out every two or three days, bring to a boil and cook for a few minutes to prevent spoilage.

LAMB, VEAL, PORK, ETC.

The above is the basic meat stock and is changed from beef to lamb or beef to pork or beef to veal by simply substituting the different meats—and, most important—their corresponding bones.

POULTRY STOCK

4 quarts water
1 - 5 pound chicken, quartered
(or equal amount of leftover turkey, including carcass)
1½ pounds combination of giblets, backs, necks and wings
8 peppercorns, crushed
1 onion, chopped
1 parsnip, scraped or chopped
2 celery stalks, including tops
2 carrots, scraped or chopped
2 leeks, white part only
1 parsley root
2 tablespoons butter
1 tablespoon vegetable oil
1 tablespoon salt
bouquet garni

Reserving vegetables, place chicken, bouquet garni, salt, pepper and water in pot and bring to boil. Place all vegetables in a heavy iron skillet with the butter and oil and stir-cook over low heat until onion is transparent and carrot is soft. Place in blender with about a cup of the warm liquid from the stockpot and completely liquefy. Add several more cups of liquid from stockpot and blend. Add blended mixture to stockpot and bring to boil. Remove what scum rises to top, partially cover and simmer for about 3 hours, skimming off fat as you go along (chicken may be removed after about 2 hours and set aside for salads, or crepe-filling). After simmer time is over, uncover pot and allow to cool. Refrigerate overnight. The next day, carefully remove all hardened fat and reheat. Cool and refrigerate in sealed containers. Entire stockpot may be refrigerated, but it should be brought to a boil once every 2 or 3 days.

BASIC FISH STOCK

6 cups water
3 pounds fish trimmings (bones, heads, fins, etc.)
1 onion, chopped
1 celery stalk, chopped
1 carrot, scraped and chopped
2 cups dry white wine
6 peppercorns, crushed
bouquet garni
1 tablespoon butter
1 tablespoon vegetable oil

Heat butter and oil in iron skillet (the oil keeps the butter from burning), add vegetables and stir-fry a few minutes (until onion is transparent). Liquefy and place with water and all other ingredients in stockpot. Bring to boil. Reduce heat and simmer for about 45 minutes, constantly skimming off any scum that surfaces. Strain through cheesecloth and allow to completely cool before refrigerating.

VEGETABLE STOCK

7 cups water
2 cups onion, chopped
1 cup leeks, minced
½ cup celery root, chopped
½ cup turnip, chopped
1 cup carrots, chopped
1 cup cabbage, chopped
2 peppercorns, crushed
3 tablespoons butter
1 tablespoon vegetable oil
bouquet garni

Stir-fry vegetables in combination butter and oil about three or four minutes (until onion becomes transparent). Place in blender with a little of the water and liquefy the whole works. Add mixture to water in stockpot, stir and add other ingredients. Bring to boil, lower heat and simmer about 2½ hours. Season to taste.

NOTES

•

three

COLD FRUIT SOUPS OR DESSERTS

We consider the commercialization of farmlands by corporate growers one of the great crimes of the past half-century because they have stolen from us a number of luscious fruits and vegetables. If the products haven't been endowed with the ability to survive days and/or weeks in the supermarket bins, they have simply been banished. Such fruits as the delicate and delicious satsuma plum are now harvested (where grown) for preserves only. Certain apples are no longer available and the marvelous persimmon—which must be picked at a certain advanced stage of ripeness to even taste like a persimmon—is quickly disappearing. Real tomatoes, of course, have already gone the way of the dinosaur. The modern tomato has been cross-bred and double-cross-bred so that it can be picked green by machines, dumped in trucks like rocks and later turned red (but certainly not ripe) by a gas which removes the chlorophyll.

The only answer is to grow your own and no matter whether you live in an apartment or have several acres, it is possible with most items. Container gardens on balconies can provide most of your vegetables and herbs and even fruits from dwarf varieties of trees. Even though we are fortunate to live on a hillside with more than an acre of land, we are turning to containers for our produce because of the animals. Racoons love avocados, rabbits

15

love vegetables and gophers love anything that grows. We are hopeful this strategy will also bring back our lost love for certain animals.

Some years ago, when it became obvious that the satsuma plum indeed was gone, we bought a small tree. We nourished it, doted on it and watched it with growing anticipation. Our nurseryman told us to expect only one plum the first year and, true to his word, it slowly appeared and took shape. Each day, we would check it for size and firmness. It was like waiting for a baby. Finally, it was almost ready and the decision was made to pick the plum the next day. That evening, we were sitting in the living room and looked up to see a small boy riding by the house on his bicycle. As he passed the tree, he reached up, snatched the plum and pedaled off. We only hope he enjoyed the fruit of our labor.

Anyway, enough of life's little tragedies. Let's move on to one of our favorite provinces of the soup kingdom—cold fruit soups. We are at a loss to understand the treatment accorded these delicate dishes by most cookbooks and particularly by restaurants. How often do you see a cold cherry soup as the "de jour" offering? And, how often have you found anything but something called "Scandinavian Fruit Soup" in a cookbook? Well, we're here to cure that problem right now.

The beauty of cold fruit soups is that they can also, with a dash of sweetening, double as desserts. That's the simple formula: omit sweetening for soup, add it for desserts. What we generally do if we opt for the latter is to pour the liquid into parfait glasses and chill in the freezer for about a half-hour before serving.

With all this buildup, you might wonder why this section appears so small, consisting of only about a dozen actual recipes. The answer is that there is *one* basic fruit soup recipe and all you do to make it different is to change the fruit. For instance, we have used the basic recipe in the lead-off item, cold cherry soup. To instantly turn it into an Indian red peach soup (our favorite), omit the cherries and substitute peaches. The same is true for apricots, grapes, apples or what-have-you. Obviously, as in the case of peaches or apricots, you most likely would not want to include the skins. So, after the fruit has cooled (before being placed in blender), simply peel them with a small knife.

COLD CHERRY SOUP OR DESSERT
(BASIC FRUIT SOUP RECIPE)

2 pounds cherries, stemmed
1½ cups water
1½ cups dry white wine
½ cup sugar or ⅓ cup honey
2 tablespoons cornstarch or 1 tablespoon arrowroot
1 pint heavy (whipping) cream

Bring water, wine and sweetening to boil. Add cherries, cover and simmer for about 15 minutes. Remove cherries with a slotted spoon and allow to cool. Mix cornstarch or arrowroot in a little water until dissolved. Stir into wine-water mixture and stir-cook until thickened (about 15 minutes). Pit cherries (when cooked, a gentle squeeze between your fingertips will pop the pits right out). Combine with about a cup of the sauce and puree in blender. Add remaining sauce and cream, mix well and chill before serving. Garnish each bowl with either fresh cherries or with several cooked cherries saved from the blender.

CURRIED APPLE SOUP

2 large apples, peeled, cored and cubed
1 large onion, coarsely chopped
4 tablespoons butter
2½ cups chicken stock
1 tablespoon curry powder
2 tablespoons cornstarch or 1 tablespoon arrowroot
⅔ cup heavy cream
2 egg yolks
juice of ½ lemon
salt and freshly ground black pepper

Melt butter in heavy saucepan, add onion and cook until transparent. Stir in stock and curry powder. Add cornstarch or arrowroot after dissolving in a little cold water. Bring mixture to boil and simmer for about 10 minutes. In separate pan, heat cream and add egg yolks. Stir mixture gradually into hot soup. Place one apple in blender, add a little of the soup, salt and pepper and blend until smooth. Slowly stir into remaining soup. Chill and serve with garnish of the second diced apple and watercress leaves.

PERLA MEYERS' AVOCADO VELOUTE
(DELICIOUS HOT OR COLD)

1½ ripe avocado
6 tablespoons butter
1 cup finely minced scallions (green part only)
2 garlic cloves, mashed
juice of 1 lemon
4 tablespoons flour
6 cups chicken stock
salt and freshly ground white pepper
3 egg yolks
1 cup heavy cream
few drops Tabasco

GARNISH: Freshly minced fresh chives and ½ cup heavy cream, whipped and slightly salted.

Melt 2 tablespoons butter in a small, heavy saucepan. Add scallions and garlic and cook uncovered over very low heat about 5 minutes or until soft, but not browned. Remove them and place in blender. Add to blender mashed pulp of 1 avocado. Sprinkle with half of the lemon juice and blend at high speed until pureed. Set aside. Melt remaining butter in heavy large saucepan, add flour and stir-cook mixture for about 2 minutes. Heat stock and whisk into butter-flour mixture until soup is slightly thickened and smooth. Season with salt and pepper and simmer, partially covered, about 35 minutes. Combine egg yolks, Tabasco and cream and blend well. Fold avocado puree into this mixture and then pour into soup, stirring constantly. Heat, but do not boil. Cube remaining avocado, sprinkle with remaining lemon juice and add to soup just before serving. This soup may be varied when serving cold by garnishing with fresh chervil.

GENA LARSON'S AVOCADO-ASPARAGUS SOUP

1 cup asparagus spears, cut and lightly steamed
1 large avocado, cubed
2 cups half-and-half
½ teaspoon mixed herb seasoning
¼ teaspoon dill weed
½ teaspoon sea salt
¼ teaspoon dried onion flakes

Blend all ingredients in blender until smooth. Heat and serve garnished with chopped chives, parsley sprigs or curry powder.

AVOCADO GAZPACHO

2 large avocados
1 cup sour cream
½ cup milk
1 cup fresh tomato juice
1 cup tomato sauce
3 tablespoons fresh lemon juice
1 garlic clove, finely minced
1 cucumber, peeled, seeded and minced
1 tomato, peeled, seeded and minced
1 bay leaf
½ teaspoon Tabasco sauce
salt and pepper to taste

Whip sour cream then beat in milk, tomato juice, tomato sauce, 2 tablespoons of the lemon juice and the garlic. Add cucumbers, tomato, and bay leaf, Tabasco, salt and pepper and chill thoroughly to blend flavors. After chilled, remove bay leaf. Mash avocados with remaining lemon juice and blend with chilled mixture. Serve garnished with additional peeled, seeded and diced cucumber and tomato.

AVOCADO-PINEAPPLE SOUP

1 large ripe avocado
½ cup crushed canned pineapple, drained
1 cup chicken stock
1½ tablespoon fresh lemon juice
1 teaspoon each minced parsley, chives and chervil
salt and pepper to taste

In blender, puree all ingredients except herbs. Chill at least one hour and serve garnished with the herbs, garlic croutons and an additional avocado, diced and rubbed with lemon juice.

CANTALOUPE SOUP

1 large cantaloupe
2½ cups milk
5 tablespoons butter
2 teaspoons sugar or 1½ teaspoon honey
1 teaspoon grated lemon rind
1 teaspoon fresh lemon juice
1 teaspoon white rum
salt, pepper and ginger to taste

Cut cantaloupe, remove seeds and make balls for garnish (about 2 for each bowl). Dice remaining cantaloupe and saute in heavy pan with butter and sweetening. Add lemon rind, salt, pepper and ginger and stir-cook 2 minutes. Add milk, bring to boil and simmer about 10 minutes. Puree entire mixture in blender. Chill for at least 1 hour before serving. Stir in lemon juice and rum and garnish with melon balls and fresh mint leaves.

COLD LEMON SOUP

3 cups chicken stock
1½ tablespoons small tapioca
2 egg yolks
1½ tablespoons fresh lemon juice
¾ teaspoon grated lemon peel
¾ cup heavy cream

Bring the stock to a boil in the top of a double boiler. Slowly stir in tapioca and cook for about 4 minutes. Reduce heat and simmer, partially covered, for an additional 5 minutes. In a separate bowl, combine egg yolks, lemon juice, lemon rind, a little salt and, if you like, a little Tabasco sauce. Add heavy cream and mix well. Add 1 tablespoon stock to cream mixture and stir. Add stock, stirring all the while, spoon by spoon. Return entire mixture to top of double boiler and stir over low heat until thickened. Cool, chill and serve. If too thick, stir in additional lemon juice or a little light cream.

ORIENTAL MUSKMELON SOUP

8 cups chicken stock
3 slices fresh ginger root
2 pounds muskmelon, diced
½ pound fresh or ¼ pound dried mushrooms, diced
1 teaspoon tangerine peel, grated
½ cup water chestnuts, diced
½ cup bamboo shoots, diced
1 raw chicken breast, skinned and diced
½ cup ham diced

Heat stock and add ginger root. Bring to boil and simmer for about 30 minutes. Add melon, mushrooms, tangerine peel, water chestnuts and bamboo shoots. Cover, bring to boil, reduce heat and simmer for 45 minutes. Add chicken and simmer an additional 20 minutes. Garnish with ham, Chinese parsley, if available, and a little dry sherry if you like.

WATERMELON SOUP

½ medium-sized watermelon
1½ cup Rhine or other white wine
⅔ cup sugar or ½ cup honey
4 slices lemon or lime
1 vanilla bean
¾ cup water

Cut melon and make about a dozen balls from the seedless portion. Place in bowl with wine and chill. Heat water in heavy saucepan and add citrus slices, sweetening, vanilla bean and simmer, covered, for about 20 minutes. Remove citrus and vanilla. Seed and cube 3 cups melon, place in blender along with the sweetened water and blend until smooth. Combine mixture with melon ball-wine mixture, chill for at least 1 hour and serve garnished with fresh minced mint.

ORANGE JUICE—WINE SOUP

1½ cups water
1 cup fresh-squeezed orange juice
¼ cup honey
1 teaspoon orange peel, grated
3 tablespoons cornstarch or 2 tablespoons arrowroot
½ teaspoon mace
½ teaspoon salt
2 cups dry white wine

Reserving wine and cornstarch, place all ingredients in heavy saucepan and bring to boil, stirring constantly. Dissolve cornstarch or arrowroot in a little cold water and stir into mixture and continue cooking until thickened. Remove from heat and stir in wine. Chill, covered, for at least 2 hours before serving. Serve garnished with fresh mint leaves.

SCANDINAVIAN FRUIT SOUP

1 cup dried apples
1 cup dried peaches
1 cup dried apricots
½ cup seedless raisins
½ cup pitted prunes
2 quarts water
½ cup currant jelly
1 orange, sliced
1 lemon, sliced
2 tablespoons tapioca

Soak dried fruit overnight in water. Add jelly, fresh fruits and tapioca and cook for about 30 minutes. Chill for at least 2 hours before serving and garnish with fresh mint leaves or spoonsful of whipped cream.

● **NOTES** ●

four

HEARTY MEALS IN A POT

We have some friends who are extremely busy people, active in community affairs, politics, movements of all kinds, and are invariably overbooked. The male partner has been early for only one meeting in his entire life—and that was because he made a mistake on his calendar and arrived 23 hours early, thinking, of course, that he was an hour late. We had them to dinner several years ago and we had prepared one of those meals where timing is of the utmost importance. We had asked them for 7 p.m., figuring to eat at 8 — not 8:10, you understand, but at 8. They dawdled in at 9:15 and we served and ate a thoroughly destroyed meal through clenched teeth. About a year passed and we ran into them at a gathering of some kind and, without thinking, asked them to dinner. They checked their calendars and found a mutually free day about two months ahead. Well, 60 days is a long time and we completely forgot about it. Early on the date of the dinner, we received a call from some other friends inviting us to join them for a casual dinner and an evening of bridge. We accepted and had a marvelous time, arriving home about midnight. There on the door was a note from our dinner guests. We were naturally horrified at what we had done and Mike went straight to the telephone. "Max," he said, "this is Mike Spencer..." and before he could get his apology out, Max began his. "I'm really sorry, Mike, but we got tied up at the board meeting and I want you to know that we don't blame you for leaving after what happened last time." They thought their tardiness had so angered us that we had stalked out of our own house to teach them a lesson. It might have, too, if we hadn't told them the truth.

Anyway, if you have friends who are habitually tardy or people dropping by after a football game or other guests coming at no set time for a meal, soups are for you—especially those in this chapter. While all soups can be the central part of a meal, surrounded by salad and bread or rolls, those entered here are particularly hearty. They can be prepared long ahead of time and simply reheated when everyone has finally arrived.

BEEF RAGOUT

3 pounds beef chuck, cut into chunks
3 tablespoons butter
3 tablespoons oil
3 onions, minced
2 garlic cloves, minced
2 tablespoons tomato paste
1 teaspoon marjoram
1 teaspoon paprika
salt and freshly ground pepper
2 pounds fresh mushrooms
2 tablespoons fresh dill
1 cup sour cream

Saute the meat in the oil and butter and remove the meat from the pan. Add the onion and garlic and cook until they are tender. Add the tomato paste, marjoram and paprika. Return the meat to the casserole, add mushrooms and seasonings and place in a 350° oven. Cook for 2 hours or until the meat is tender. If the sauce seems to be too thin, remove the meat and reduce the liquid over high heat. Mix the dill and sour cream and serve.

CHICKEN STRACCIATELLA

6 chicken legs with thighs
8 cups chicken stock
1½ cup uncooked vermicelli or other thin pasta
2 eggs
1½ tablespoon semolina
3 tablespoons grated Parmesan or Romano cheese
salt and pepper to taste

Bake chicken legs in oven until done, basting with butter. Heat chicken stock to boiling point and add pasta. Cook until pasta is done. Remove about a cup of the stock and cool. When cool, combine with eggs, semolina and cheese and mix well. Slowly add to stock-pasta mixture. Add cooked chicken and simmer about 10 minutes. Serve in large bowls with whole chicken leg in each.

VARIATION

1. Add 1½ cups cooked, diced green beans to soup before adding egg mixture.

2. Add 1½ cups cooked peas to soup before adding egg mixture.

JOAN HEWETT'S CHICKEN POT

3½ pounds frying chicken, cut up
2½ cups water
4 tomatoes, chopped
¾ cup ham, diced
1 onion, chopped
⅓ cup olive oil
2 cloves garlic, minced
1½ cups uncooked rice
¾ green pepper, chopped
1 bay leaf
2½ teaspoon salt
½ teaspoon cumin seed
½ teaspoon saffron

Brown chicken pieces in olive oil. Add water and tomatoes and simmer for about 20 minutes. Add remaining ingredients, cover, and simmer until rice is done. For thinner, soupier dish, add 3 cups chicken stock with the rice.

CHILI BEEF SOUP

5 cups water
5 cups chicken or vegetable stock
1 onion, chopped
2 green peppers, chopped
2 cloves garlic, minced
1½ pound ground beef
1 pound tomatoes, peeled and pureed in blender
4 cups dried kidney beans
chili powder to taste

Melt butter in heavy saucepan and stir-fry onions, peppers and garlic until onion is transparent. Add ground beef and stir-fry until cooked. Pour over stock-water mixture, add tomatoes and beans and simmer, slowly, for about 3 hours. Stir in chili powder to taste. (Be careful: a little goes a long way.) Garnish with fresh-chopped onion and grated cheddar cheese.

CREOLE STEW

5 cups water
5 cups beef stock
2 pounds stewing meat
2 onions, chopped
3 tablespoons butter
1 pound fresh tomatoes, pureed in blender
½ cup dry red wine
2½ cups uncooked rice
bouquet garni

Melt butter in heavy skillet and stir-fry onions until transparent. Remove onions and brown meat chunks. Reserving rice, pour over all other ingredients and simmer, covered, for 1½ hours. Add rice and continue cooking until rice is done. Remove garni and serve garnished with fresh parsley sprigs.

VARIATION

As with any stew, you can use your imagination when it comes to ingredients. Use potatoes instead of rice; add a couple of peeled and chopped carrots, etc. You can't hurt this dish.

LAMB STEW

5 cups lamb or beef stock
5 cups water
3 pounds lamb, cut like stew meat
2 onions, chopped
4 carrots, chopped
2 turnips, diced
2 pounds, potatoes, peeled and diced
bouquet garni with ¼ teaspoon rosemary added

Melt butter and stir-fry onions, carrots and turnips until onion is transparent. Using a slotted spoon, remove the vegetables and add the meat. Stir-fry until browned on all sides. Put vegetables back in pan, pour in the stock-water mixture, potatoes and garni and simmer covered, about 2 hours.

MEATBALL SKILLET

1 pound ground meat
½ cup bread crumbs
1 egg
1 cup beef stock
1 cup water, or more if needed
1 onion, chopped
2 potatoes, cut into chunks
4 carrots, cut into strips
bunch of green onions
1 teaspoon salt
½ teaspoon pepper
1 cup fresh mushrooms

Combine the ground meat, bread crumbs, and egg and shape into balls. Brown in butter. Add beef stock, water and the vegetables and simmer for half an hour.

FISH AND NOODLE CASSEROLE

2 pounds fresh fish (halibut or cod), boned
2 cups uncooked vermicelli or other thin noodle
2 cups grated cheddar cheese
3 tablespoons fresh lemon juice
3 tablespoons butter
3 tablespoons flour
3 cups milk
5 cups fish or chicken stock
bouquet garni

Heat stock, add garni and simmer about 30 minutes. Add fish and cook until done (it will flake). Remove fish and set aside. Add noodles and cook until tender (about 10 minutes). Make a paste with melted butter and flour and stir into pot. Remove garni, add cheese and stir until cheese melts. Add milk, lemon juice and fish and heat just enough to heat the fish. Garnish with fresh parsley sprigs.

POT-AU-FEU

1 meaty ham bone
1 meaty lamb bone
1 meaty beef bone
5 cups water
5 cups beef stock
½ cup dried lima beans
½ cup dried navy beans
½ cup dried split peas
2 tablespoons uncooked rice
2 onions, chopped
1 celery stalk, chopped
2 tablespoons parsley, minced
1 cup tomato puree
bouquet garni

Heat water-stock combination and place all ingredients into large pot. Cover and simmer 4 hours. Remove bones from pot, cut off meat and put meat into pot after skimming off any scum that has risen to the top. Remove garni, reheat and serve garnished with chopped chives or fresh sprigs of parsley.

TOMATO-BEEF GRATIN

3 cups water
3 cups beef stock
1½ pounds ground beef
2 onions, chopped
3 tablespoons butter
2 pounds tomatoes, peeled and chopped
5 tablespoons bread crumbs
½ cup grated Romano, Parmesan or Cheddar cheese
2 tablespoons parsley, minced
⅛ teaspoon rosemary

Melt butter in heavy skillet and saute onions until transparent. Add meat and stir-fry until done. Add tomatoes and stock mixture and cook, covered, until half of the stock has cooked down. Sprinkle bread crumbs and cheese over top, cover and simmer gently for an additional hour (you can also bake this dish).

CHEDDAR CHEESE SOUP

2 medium carrots, scraped and minced
2 stalks celery, minced
1 onion, finely chopped
¼ cup flour
½ teaspoon salt
⅛ teaspoon white pepper
1 quart chicken broth
1 pound raw, sharp, cheddar cheese, grated
1 cup heavy cream
1 cup milk

Saute the vegetables in the butter until soft. Sprinkle with flour and mix to smooth paste. Add salt, pepper, and chicken stock. Cool and puree vegetables. Add cheese and reheat soup, do not boil. When ready to serve, add the milk and cream. Garnish with minced parsley and grated carrot.

CHEESE WINE SOUP

3 tablespoons flour
3 tablespoons butter
4½ cups hot milk
2 cloves garlic
2 cups firmly packed grated extra sharp cheddar cheese
1½ cup dry white wine or vermouth
salt and freshly ground white pepper
3 egg yolks
¼ cup heavy cream

Melt the butter and stir in the flour. Cook for 2 minutes. Whisk in the milk. Add the garlic and cook over low heat for 25 minutes, stirring frequently. Do not boil. Remove the garlic cloves and discard. Stir in the cheese and wine. Season to taste. Beat the egg yolks with the cream. Stir mixture gradually into the soup. Simmer for 5 minutes. Serve garnished with grated cheese and nutmeg.

WINE GAZPACHO

2 pounds tomatoes, seeded, peeled and diced
1 cup minced onion
2 pressed garlic cloves
½ cup peeled, seeded and diced cucumber
1 - 3¼ ounce can pitted black olives, halved
4 drops Tabasco
½ teaspoon salt
¼ teaspoon black pepper
2 tablespoons olive oil
⅛ teaspoon sugar
1 cup dry red wine
extra diced vegetables
minced parsley
herbed croutons

Combine all ingredients and chill. Serve with extra diced vegetables, parsley and herb croutons.

MIDDLE EAST YOGURT SOUP

½ cup pearl barley
2 cups water
4 cups cold water
2 cups yogurt
4 eggs
2 tablespoons flour
2 tablespoons minced onion
2 tablespoons butter
salt
juice from 1 large lemon
minced mint
minced fresh coriander

Cook barley in 2 cups water for 1 hour, adding more water if needed. Drain. Combine cold water and yogurt. Beat eggs and flour and combine in yogurt. Bring slowly to simmer and cook 3 minutes. Add barley, onions, butter and salt to taste; simmer 1 more minute. Remove from heat and add lemon juice. Adjust seasonings to taste and pass minced mint and coriander. This may be served hot or cold.

•   **NOTES**   •

five

SOUPS FROM YOUR VICTORY GARDEN

We were once held culinary prisoners for several days at one of the most romantic hide-aways in the world, a hotel built into the bluffs along California's roughest coastal area. The sea is so threatening and the weather so unpredictable that even the most experienced fishermen stay away. The road winding past the establishment rims sheer cliffs and snakes up and down and around the violent surf without so much as a single guard rail or lane marker to aid or protect the traveler. And, it is frequently and without warning engulfed in heavy, bone-chilling fog.

The rooms have no televisions and no telephones and all boast spectacular views and Japanese-style bathtubs for two. It is a place for lovers, a place where couples can share in nature and in themselves . . . walks along the cliffs, intimate talks, a little wine, maybe, and as we said, love.

We, however, were accompanied by our then-nine-year-old and found ourselves waking in the mornings to the sound of cards being shuffled and mournful pleas for someone to play Old Maid or Gin Rummy or anything to pass the time until we could get out of that dreadful, boring place.

It was neither dreadful nor boring to us until we reached the dining room where we were to discover that at the very time we were viewing Mother Nature in her glory through the huge plate

35

glass windows, her bounty was taking a severe beating in the kitchen. Frozen foods, thawed and overcooked, dominated the menu. Salads were limp and tasteless; the bread white. Worst of all, the nearest restaurant was 20 miles away—up that road!— and there was no way of knowing that the food would be any better even if we got there. We asked the waiter what was good. "Nothing!" was the blunt reply. We were stuck; prisoners at $35 a day.

We ordered sparingly and as selectively as we could, rejecting with knowing glances at one another any suggestion of "soup de jour." Indeed, thought we, more likely "soup de can"— until we heard the couple at the next table raving about it. We hesitatingly tried a cup, then bowls, then buckets as we cancelled our dinner orders. It was exquisite, it was marvelous, it was carrot soup made with personal and loving care in that same kitchen by a chef who was allowed to tinker with soups, if not with the entrees. He somehow had stumbled across the little-known fact that the vegetable family encompasses more than just potatoes, onions and beans. We had carrot soup one day, water-cress the next and even supped—or, more properly, souped—on such delights as bell pepper soup, cold broccoli and creamy cabbage, in between games of Old Maid and Gin Rummy. His stockpot, combined with the brisk but clean air and the crashing of the surf, salvaged our holiday.

Artichokes, asparagus, beans, beets, broccoli, cabbage, carrots, cauliflower, celery, chard, corn, cucumbers, eggplant, garlic, kale, leeks, mushrooms, onions, parsley, parsnips, peas, peppers, potatoes, pumpkin, spinach, squash, sweet potatoes, tomatoes, turnips, watercress and even peanuts are all of the vegetable family and all make super soups, many of which can be served either hot or cold, before meals or *as* meals. Suffice to say that it would be physically impossible to include all soups involving all vegetables in this chapter. Remember, though, that once you have a basic recipe, interchanging vegetables is no prob-lem. Experiment . . . and enjoy.

HOT VEGETABLE SOUPS

BASIC VEGETABLE-BEEF SOUP

3 pounds stew meat, cut into ½ inch chunks
8 cups water
2 cups canned tomatoes with liquid
½ cup onion, chopped
1 cup celery, diced
1 cup carrots, diced
1 cup potatoes, cubed
1 cup cabbage, chopped
2 whole bay leaves
2 teaspoons Worcestershire sauce
¼ teaspoon chili powder
salt and pepper to taste

Brown meat in oil. Add water, canned tomatoes, onion and seasonings and simmer covered for about 1½ hours. Add vegetables and simmer an additional hour. Remove bay leaves and serve.

ALSATIAN VEGETABLE SOUP

1 cup dry white beans
2 tablespoons butter
2 onions, chopped
4 large garlic cloves, minced
3 carrots, peeled and quartered
2 celery stalks, cut into chunks
4 leeks, sliced (white part only)
4 medium potatoes, peeled and cut into chunks
3 small white turnips, peeled and quartered
bouquet garni
1 ham bone
1 pound lean blanched bacon
10 cups beef stock
1 large cabbage, shredded (preferably Savoy)
salt
6 crushed peppercorns

(continued)

Soak the beans overnight in cold water. Drain and parboil for 15 minutes in salted water. Drain and reserve. In a large heavy pot melt butter, add onions and garlic and cook for about 3 minutes. Add the potatoes, leeks, celery, carrots, turnips, beans and bouquet garni. Cover with the beef stock, salt and pepper and bring to a boil. Add the ham bone and bacon. Cover partially and cook the soup over medium heat for 1 hour.

FLEMISH VEGETABLE SOUP

2 carrots
2 leeks (white part only)
2 cups fresh spinach
1 head Boston lettuce
6 cups chicken stock
1 parsnip, peeled, cut in half lengthwise,
then cut into 1 inch pieces
3 small turnips, peeled and cubed
2 small potatoes, peeled and cubed
4 tablespoons butter
4 tablespoons flour
salt and freshly ground white pepper
½ cup heavy cream

Peel and dice carrots, wash leeks, spinach and lettuce. Cut the lettuce into large chunks. Heat the chicken stock and add the vegetables, except for spinach and lettuce. Cook until barely tender, about 20 minutes. Strain the stock and keep warm. Reserve the vegetables. Melt the butter and add the flour. Cook without browning for 2 or 3 minutes. Add the warm stock and whisk until the soup gets thicker and is smooth. Add the spinach and lettuce. Season with salt and pepper and add the reserved vegetables. Cook for 5 minutes. Just before serving, add cream and garnish with parsley and chives.

FARMER'S VEGETABLE SOUP

½ onion, diced
2 leeks (white part only), diced
1 turnip, diced
2 carrots, diced
1 teaspoon salt
pinch sugar
3 tablespoons butter
6 cups beef stock
1 potato, thinly sliced
6 tablespoons bacon, diced and blanched

Sprinkle the diced vegetables with salt and sugar, simmer for 5 minutes in butter in a covered pan. Add stock, cover and simmer 50 minutes. Add potato and bacon and simmer for 20 minutes or until potatoes are done.

BASIC FRENCH ONION SOUP

5 cups onions, sliced
1 tablespoon oil
3 tablespoons butter
1 teaspoon salt
¼ teaspoon sugar
3 tablespoons flour
2 quarts beef stock
½ cup dry white wine
salt and pepper to taste
3 tablespoons cognac
rounds of hard toasted French bread
1 - 2 cups grated Swiss or Parmesan cheese

Cook the onions over low heat in the butter and oil in a heavy-bottomed saucepan for 15 minutes. Uncover, raise the heat to moderate and stir in the salt and sugar. Cook 30 to 40 minutes until the onions are a rich golden brown. Stir in the flour and cook for 3 minutes. Blend in the boiling stock. Add the wine, and season to taste. Simmer partially covered for 30 or 40 minutes more. When ready to serve, reheat to simmer and stir in the cognac. Pour over bread rounds in bowls and pass the cheese separately.

MR. BARHYDT'S FRENCH ONION SOUP

If you happen to watch the CBS television morning news, you will oft-times hear anchorman Hughes Rudd introduce a funny item with these words: "And, here's a Frank Barhydt story . . ." Mr. Barhydt is an old Kansas City cronie of Mr. Rudd's and his son and daughter-in-law are special friends of ours. The senior Mr. Barhydt is a fancy cook, of sorts, and prides himself on his homemade wines, even though the Kansas City Star once described his wine cellar as a "well-kept dump." His daughter-in-law, Judy, introduced us to this soup and we feel honor-bound to place the blame where it belongs.

5 medium onions, sliced and quartered
2 cups chicken stock
2 cups beef stock
5 tablespoons butter
3 pinches marjoram
1 teaspoon freshly ground black pepper
1½ teaspoons Dijon mustard
1 jigger bourbon or scotch
¼ cup red or white wine
2 tablespoons flour
1 teaspoon salt

Poach onions in butter and a little stock until clear but not brown. Add salt, pepper and mustard. Heat stocks, wine and booze to boiling point. Sprinkle onions with flour and work to a smooth paste. Add stock-booze mixture. Pour into oven-proof bowls, top with chunks of French bread and grated Parmesan or Romano cheese and heat under broiler until cheese bubbles. (Soup can be kept, Mr. Barhydt insists, for "as long as you wish" in a 200° oven.)

CREAM OF TOMATO SOUP

3 pounds fresh tomatoes
4 tablespoons butter
1 onion, chopped
3 tablespoons flour
1 tablespoon vegetable oil
2 cups water
2 cups chicken stock
1 tablespoon honey or powdered sugar
½ pint heavy cream
bouquet garni with 1 teaspoon each marjoram and dill added
salt and pepper to taste

Bring water and stock to boil and add whole tomatoes. Cook for 1 minute, remove with slotted spoon, drain, peel and chunk. Heat half the butter and all the oil in large cast-iron skillet. Add onion and stir-fry until onions are transparent. Add remaining butter, sprinkle on flour and stir-fry until mixture thickens. Add tomatoes, then stir in boiling mixture of stock and water. Add bouquet garni, salt and pepper and honey or sugar. Cover and simmer for about 35 minutes. Remove bouquet garni and cool soup. Puree in blender, slowly add cream, reheat and serve. Garnish with grated Cheddar cheese, croutons, fresh parsley or—and don't laugh until you've tried it—hot buttered popcorn.

VARIATIONS

1. After puree/blender process and before adding cream, add 1½ cups uncooked rice, return to heat and cook covered for an additional 30 minutes or until rice is done and you have tomato-rice soup.
2. For plain tomato soup, simply omit the cream.

TOMATO BORSCHT

1 cup chopped onions
2 tablespoons butter
1 ½ cups tomato juice, preferably fresh
1 ½ cups beef stock
½ teaspoon salt
½ teaspoon sugar
1 small head cabbage, finely shredded
½ cup cooked meat (beef or chicken)
black pepper
whipped sour cream

Saute onion in butter until soft and slightly browned. Add tomato juice, stock, salt and sugar. Cover, bring to boil, reduce heat and simmer for 30 minutes. Bring back to boil and add cabbage. Cook just until cabbage is tender. Reheat with meat and adjust seasonings. Sprinkle with black pepper and top with sour cream.

CREAM OF MUSHROOM SOUP

2 pounds mushrooms, thinly sliced
¾ cups carrots, chopped
¾ cups onions, sliced
¼ cup celery, chopped
1 quart chicken stock
2 cups heavy cream
4 tablespoons minced parsley
6 tablespoons flour or 2 tablespoons arrowroot

Melt butter in heavy cast-iron pot and stir-fry mushrooms until done. With a slotted spoon, remove mushrooms, leaving as much of the liquid as possible in the pot. Add carrots, onions and celery and stir-fry until onions are transparent. Place in blender with about 2 cups of the chicken stock and liquefy. Place mixture into pot, add flour or arrowroot slowly, stir-frying until paste is formed. Slowly add chicken stock, stirring all along. Then add mushrooms, stir, add cream very slowly, continuing to stir, and serve. Garnish with croutons or grated carrot or whatever you happen to like.

VARIATION

If you prefer a brown mushroom soup, sans the cream, simply substitute beef stock for the chicken and omit the cream.

QUICK CREAM OF MUSHROOM SOUP

1 ½ pounds fresh mushrooms
1 quart beef stock
1 cup fresh parsley, chopped
2 cups sour cream
2 tablespoons fresh lemon juice
5 tablespoons butter

Slice mushrooms thinly. Melt butter in large cast-iron pot and stir-fry mushrooms over low heat until done. Add lemon juice, parsley, cook a few minutes, add stock and heat. Gradually stir in sour cream until well blended and serve. For heavier and heartier soup, substitute heavy cream for the sour cream. Garnish with grated carrot and croutons, or whatever else strikes your fancy.

MUSHROOM AND BARLEY SOUP

4 cups chicken stock
4 cups beef stock
1 cup barley, uncooked
4 tablespoons butter
1 pound mushrooms, thinly sliced
1 medium onion, chopped
1 cup carrots, chopped
½ cup celery, chopped
3 tablespoons flour
salt and pepper to taste

Cook barley in heavy pot with stock mixture until done (about 45 minutes). In heavy skillet, melt butter, and saute mushrooms until done. Remove with slotted spoon and set aside. Add onions, carrots and celery to butter and stir-fry until onions are transparent. Puree in blender, return to skillet and add flour. Stir-fry until paste is formed. Stir into simmering liquid and add mushrooms and barley. Season to taste.

BASIC LENTIL SOUP

2 cups lentils
8 cups water
2½ pounds meaty ham hock
1 onion, diced
1 celery stalk, diced
2 carrots, diced
1 large can whole tomatoes
3 tablespoons butter
bouquet garni

Stir-fry onions, celery and carrots in butter until onion is transparent. Place in blender with a cup or so of the water and puree. Place remaining water in pot, bring to boil and slowly add vegetable puree. When well mixed, add ham hock, lentils, bouquet garni, tomatoes and spices to taste and simmer for at least 2½ hours. Remove ham hock, shave off the meat and toss meat back into pot.

VARIATIONS

The variations for this oldest-of-soups are endless. Here you can use your imagination and even let it run wild. For instance: add about 2 cups of diced potatoes 30 minutes before removing ham hock; add a cup of fresh fruit about 5 minutes before removing ham hock; add a cup or two of uncooked rice 35 minutes before removing the ham hock; add cooked chunks of sausage 5 minutes before removing ham hock (getting the idea?), etc.

•   **NOTES**   •

POTATO SOUP

1½ cups minced leeks
¼ cup minced onion
1 large garlic clove, minced
3 tablespoons minced carrot
4 tablespoons butter
4 cups chicken stock
1½ cups diced potatoes
½ cup heavy cream
salt
white pepper

Saute leeks, onion, garlic and carrot in butter until soft. Add stock and potatoes. Cover, bring to a boil, reduce heat and simmer until potatoes are tender. Puree in blender. Add cream, reheat without boiling and season with salt and pepper. If too thick, thin with half and half. Before serving you may add 3 tablespoons dry sherry or vermouth.

SWEET POTATO SOUP

1 tablespoon bacon fat
3 stalks celery, chopped
1 cup onion, chopped
1 pound sweet potatoes, peeled and sliced
5 cups chicken stock
½ teaspoon salt
¼ teaspoon freshly ground black pepper

Saute vegetables in bacon fat for 5 minutes. Add stock, cover and bring to a boil. Reduce heat and simmer until soft. Puree in blender and reheat. Season to taste with salt, pepper and nutmeg. Garnish with sour cream.

LEEK SOUP

6 thinly sliced leeks with ⅔ of tops removed,
saving the very tender portions for garnish
1 cup potato, peeled and thinly sliced
4 cups chicken stock
½ teaspoon celery seed
1 teaspoon seasoned salt
1 cup milk
2 tablespoons butter
2 tablespoons flour
1 cup half-and-half or ½ cup heavy cream
½ cup minced parsley

Combine leeks, potato, stock, celery seed, and salt in top of double boiler. Cover and cook for 20 minutes until the vegetables are tender. Add milk. Place over boiling water. Stir the butter into the flour, add ¼ cup of the cooking soup, stir until smooth and return to soup. Add half-and-half, cook and stir for 3 minutes, do not boil. Garnish with parsley, minced leek tops and grated cheese.

SPLIT PEA SOUP

3 quarts water
1½ pounds ham hock
2 pounds fresh split peas
3 leeks (white part only), diced
1 celery root, diced and peeled
2 onions, diced
1 cup celery tops (include leaves), chopped
2½ teaspoons salt
1 teaspoon fresh-ground black pepper
½ pound ham, diced

Cook hock in water for about 2½ hours, constantly skimming scum from top. Remove bone. Take about ⅓ of the remaining water and place in separate saucepan. Add peas and cook for about 40 minutes, stirring constantly. With the exception of the ham, add all remaining ingredients and simmer an additional half-hour. Puree in blender. Place ham and blender mix into stock, heat and serve.

PEA POD SOUP

1 cup sliced leeks
3 tablespoons butter
3 tablespoons flour
1 pound fresh green peas
4 cups hot water
1½ teaspoon salt
1 large potato, peeled and sliced
1½ cups water
1 large sliced scallion or shallot
6 - 8 outside leaves of Boston lettuce, chopped
¼ teaspoon salt
1 cup milk
salt and pepper to taste
¼ cup heavy or sour cream
1 - 4 tablespoons soft butter

Cook the leeks slowly in butter, covered 8 to 10 minutes. Set aside. Shell the peas and set aside (you should have about a cup). Wash pods and chop. Stir the chopped pods into the leeks, cover and cook slowly for 10 minutes. Blend the flour into the pea pods and stir for 1 minute. Remove from heat, blend in the cup of water, then stir in the rest along with the salt and potatoes. Simmer, partially covered, for 20 minutes or until the vegetables are tender. Add the peas, lettuce, scallion, additional water and boil for 10 minutes or until peas are tender. Puree and sieve out the pea pod fibers. Return to the pan, bring to simmer and thin out with milk if the soup seems too thick. Stir in the cream.

•   **NOTES**   •

LIMA BEAN SOUP

1 pound fresh lima beans
2 tablespoons butter
4 cups chicken stock
½ cup minced green onion
½ cup cream
½ teaspoon salt
½ teaspoon tarragon
bouquet garni

Cook beans with onion in butter until soft. Place one cup chicken stock in blender, add beans, spices and, lastly, the cream. add blender mix to stock, stir well and heat. Garnish with croutons, chives and grated fresh Romano cheese.

VARIATION FOR CURRY LOVERS

Add about a teaspoon of curry powder to the onions and beans when cooking in the butter.

BLACK BEAN SOUP

1 quart chicken stock
1 pound black beans
3 teaspoons salt
1 teaspoon pepper
1 large onion, minced
½ cup vegetable oil
10 stalks fresh sorrel
sour cream

Wash beans and soak overnight in 3 quarts water. Bring to boil with salt and pepper. Simmer for 2 hours, adding more water if necessary, until beans are tender. Puree beans and liquid in blender. Saute onion in oil for 15 minutes until golden brown. Tie the sorrel together and add to onions. Let stand about 10 minutes until leaves are wilted, stirring occasionally. Remove sorrel and discard. Add onions to puree. Thin with stock, correct seasoning and serve. Garnish with dollops of sour cream.

WHITE BEAN SOUP

1 cup dry white beans
1 large onion, finely chopped
2 tablespoons butter
2 garlic cloves, finely minced
5 cups beef stock
1 bouquet garni
1 cup heavy cream
freshly ground white pepper

Drain beans after soaking overnight in cold water. In a large pan, heat the butter. Add the onion and garlic and cook until soft but not browned. Add beans, stock, a pinch of salt, and the bouquet. Bring the mixture to a boil and cook partially covered until the beans are tender. Cool and puree in blender. Return to pan and add the cream, salt and pepper, reheat and serve.

VARIATION

Shortly before serving, add several diced sausages or chunks of smoked ham or fresh mushrooms, diced.

CHICKPEA SOUP (GARBANZO) I

2 cups chickpeas, soaked overnight
1½ quarts water
1 clove garlic, crushed
4 slices bacon, fried, drained and crumbled
1 small onion, minced
2 tablespoons tomato paste
1 teaspoon finely ground red chili
4 tablespoons sour cream

Bring the chickpeas to a boil in the water and reduce to simmer. Add the onion, bacon and garlic and stir. Slowly add the tomato paste. Make a paste of the chili and a little of the broth and return to pot. Cover and let the peas cook until tender, about 1½ hours. Serve with a spoon of sour cream on each portion.

GARBANZO SOUP II

2 cups chickpeas, soaked in 3 cups warm water, overnight
1 cup minced onion
¼ cup minced green pepper
½ cup minced leeks
2 teaspoons minced garlic
¼ cup olive oil
4 cups beef or lamb stock
1 small ham hock
1 teaspoon paprika
½ teaspoon salt
¼ teaspoon freshly ground pepper
⅛ teaspoon saffron
2 garlic sausages, sliced and sauteed in ½ teaspoon butter

Saute onion, leeks, green pepper and garlic in oil until onion is soft. Add chickpeas and their liquid, stock, ham hock, and seasonings. Cover and bring to boil. Reduce heat and simmer until chickpeas are tender. Remove ham hock and cut meat into small pieces. Return meat to soup, add sausage slices and serve with garlic croutons.

BASIL MINESTRONE

2 cups onions, chopped
2 slices bacon, diced
½ pound cooked Italian sausage, chopped
8 cups beef stock
½ cup minced parsley
1 pressed garlic clove
1 tablespoon basil, minced
¼ teaspoon cayenne pepper and ¼ teaspoon black pepper
3 cups diced potatoes
1 teaspoon salt
½ cup spaghetti
4 cups loosely packed spinach leaves

Saute onion and bacon until golden brown. Add sausage, basil, stock, garlic, cayenne and pepper, salt and potatoes. Cover, bring to a boil and cook 10 minutes. Add pasta and cook 6 minutes. Add spinach, simmer until spinach is cooked. Serve with croutons and grated cheese.

MINESTRONE, GENOVESE

2 quarts water
2 cups white beans, cooked
1 cup green beans, uncooked
3 potatoes, diced
2 tomatoes, diced
2 zucchini, diced
½ cup fresh peas
1 celery stalk, diced
1 cup shredded cabbage
3 tablespoons basil leaves, minced
3 tablespoons olive oil
2 tablespoons butter
½ teaspoon salt
3 tablespoons grated Parmesan or Romano cheese
3 cloves garlic, minced

Place last 6 ingredients in blender and make a paste. Reserve. Bring water to boil and stir in all vegetables. Simmer for about 45 minutes and gently stir in paste. Mix well and cook an additional 10 minutes.

MINESTRONE MILAN STYLE

1 teaspoon olive oil
⅛ pound salt pork, chopped
½ clove garlic, chopped
½ medium-sized onion, chopped
1 teaspoon chopped parsley
1 teaspoon chopped sage
1 teaspoon salt
½ teaspoon pepper
1 tablespoon tomato paste

3 stalks celery
2 carrots, sliced
2 potatoes, diced
2 cups cooked pea beans
¼ small cabbage, shredded
2 small zucchini, diced
1 cup shelled peas
1½ quarts beef stock
1 cup elbow macaroni

Place olive oil in a large soup pan, add salt pork, garlic, onion, parsley, sage, salt and pepper and brown. Add tomato paste diluted in ½ cup stock. Cook 5 minutes. Add all vegetables and remaining stock and simmer 45 minutes. Add macaroni, and cook 10 minutes longer. Garnish with grated cheese.

MINESTRONE TUSCAN STYLE

½ pound dry white beans
2 tablespoons oil
1 clove garlic, chopped
1 small onion, chopped
1 stalk celery, chopped
1 teaspoon rosemary
1 tablespoon tomato paste
1 small cabbage, shredded
1 zucchini, diced
1 teaspoon chopped parsley
1 teaspoon salt
½ teaspoon pepper
1 clove

Soak beans overnight. Then, boil in 3 quarts water 1 hour or until tender. While beans are cooking, place oil, garlic, onion, celery and rosemary in soup pan and brown lightly. Add tomato paste diluted by 2 tablespoons warm water and cook 5 minutes. Add cabbage, zucchini, parsley, clove, salt, pepper and beans in their liquid. Cook slowly 20 minutes. Place 2 slices toasted French bread in each soup dish, add soup and sprinkle with cheese.

CREAM OF CELERY SOUP

large bunch of celery (including stalks and tips)
1 onion, minced
2 tablespoons butter
1 quart chicken broth
salt
pepper
2 tablespoons flour
1 egg
1 pint milk or ½ pint heavy cream
bouquet garni

Remove any strings from the celery and dice stalks. Melt the butter and add celery and onion. Saute for 5 minutes. Add bouquet garni and chicken broth and cook for 1 hour. Remove the garni, add salt, pepper, milk and flour. Beat the egg until light. Pour in some of the hot soup, then stir back into the soup. Garnish with celery leaves.

CREAMED CORN SOUP

2 cups corn kernels	*1½ cups chicken stock*
1 medium onion, finely chopped	*1 quart milk*
⅓ teaspoon sugar	*2 tablespoons butter*
1 teaspoon salt	*2 tablespoons flour*
⅛ teaspoon pepper	*1 egg*

Combine vegetables in stock and simmer for 20 minutes. Add seasonings and milk and bring to a boil. Cream together the flour and butter and stir into the soup. Beat egg. Puree the soup, return to pot. Add a little stock to the egg, whisk into soup. Garnish with parsley.

SPINACH SOUP

5 cups chicken stock
¾ cup cooked rice
1½ cups finely chopped cooked spinach
⅛ teaspoon finely ground nutmeg
grated Romano or Parmesan cheese

Heat the stock to boiling, add spinach, rice and nutmeg. Reduce heat, heat through and serve topped with grated cheese.

CABBAGE SOUP

8 cups chicken stock
2 tablespoons oil
2 large onions, thinly sliced
5 garlic cloves
4 leeks (white part only) thinly sliced
4 large tomatoes, peeled and chopped
1 head Savoy cabbage, cut into chunks
2 - 3 beef shank bones
bouquet garni
1 red bell pepper, diced
salt and freshly ground white pepper

Saute the onions and garlic in oil until soft but not brown. Add leeks and cook for 5 more minutes, stirring to be sure the onions do not brown. Add the tomatoes, cabbage, bones, bouquet garni, bell pepper, salt and pepper. Add stock and bring to a boil. Skim the top, reduce heat and simmer for 2 hours, skimming occasionally. Before serving, remove the garni and greens. Remove the meat from the bones and return to soup.

CREAM OF BROCCOLI SOUP

2 - 2½ pounds broccoli
¼ cup chopped green pepper
½ cup chopped onion
2 tablespoons butter
2 tablespoons chicken stock
bouquet garni
¼ teaspoon nutmeg or ½ teaspoon curry powder
¼ teaspoon white pepper
3 egg yolks
1 cup heavy cream
salt

Reserve 12 small broccoli flowerets and chop the remaining broccoli. Saute the broccoli, onion and green pepper in butter until slightly browned. Sprinkle with the flour, cook, stirring for 3 minutes. Add stock and bouquet garni. Cook and stir until smooth and slightly thickened. Cover, bring to a boil and simmer 30 minutes, until broccoli is very soft. Discard garni. Puree in blender. Add nutmeg and pepper. Beat egg yolks and cream, whisk in ½ cup hot soup and return to soup. Reheat but don't boil. Season with salt and pepper. Garnish with slivered green onions and sour cream.

PUMPKIN SOUP

6 cups chicken stock
2 pounds fresh pumpkin, peeled and seeded
4 minced garlic cloves
1½ cups minced onion
¼ cup fresh parsley, chopped or,
2 tablespoons cilantro, if available
salt and black pepper

Combine ingredients and cook until pumpkin is tender. Puree in blender, reheat and adjust seasonings. Serve hot with the bread cubes fried in garlic, olive oil and cilantro sprigs.

CREAM OF SQUASH SOUP

2¼ cups diced yellow or banana squash
½ cup diced celery
1½ cup diced onion
2 tablespoons diced carrot
1 teaspoon basil
2 tablespoons butter
2½ cup chicken stock
1 cup half-and-half
½ cup heavy cream
¼ teaspoon sugar
⅛ teaspoon cloves
⅛ teaspoon mace
¼ teaspoon white pepper
salt
minced chives
paprika

Cook and stir vegetables and basil in butter 10 minutes. Add stock and bring to boil. Cover, reduce heat and simmer until vegetables are tender. Puree in blender, add creams and seasonings. Reheat and serve with paprika and chives. (This is also delicious served cold.)

GARLIC SOUP

12 garlic cloves
3 tablespoons butter
3 sprigs parsley
6 cups beef stock
salt and pepper
3 egg yolks
2 tablespoons oil

Melt butter and saute the garlic until soft. Add the stock, parsley, salt and pepper. Simmer for 30 minutes. Put the beaten egg yolks in a soup tureen and whisk in the oil, drop by drop. Whisk a small amount of the soup into the tureen then pour in the remaining soup through a strainer, pressing the juice out of the garlic. Garnish the croutons and freshly grated Parmesan or Romano cheese.

EGGPLANT PUREE

1 unpeeled eggplant, diced	¼ cup dry red wine
¼ cup minced mushrooms	1 tablespoon butter
2 tablespoons minced green onion and tops	1 tablespoon flour
1 minced garlic clove	¼ teaspoon sage
2 tablespoons olive oil	¾ cup heavy cream
3 cups lamb stock	salt and freshly ground pepper
pinch sugar	1 tomato, diced
1½ teaspoon tomato paste	yogurt

Saute eggplant, mushrooms, green onions and garlic in oil, covered for 10 minutes. Stir frequently. Add stock, sugar, tomato paste and wine. Cover, bring to boil and simmer until eggplant is soft. Puree in blender. In heavy pot, melt butter, sprinkle with flour and sage, cook and stir 3 minutes. Gradually add eggplant stock, cook and stir until smooth and slightly thickened. Add cream. Reheat but do not boil. Adjust seasonings. Garnish with diced tomato and yogurt.

CURRIED EGGPLANT

1 tablespoon olive oil
1 cup eggplant, peeled and cubed
¼ cup minced green onions and tops
1 tablespoon butter
½ teaspoon minced garlic
4 teaspoons flour
1 - 2 teaspoons curry powder
2 cups milk
¼ teaspoon each crushed rosemary and oregano
½ cup heavy cream
salt and freshly ground pepper

Saute eggplant in oil until golden. In saucepan, saute onion and garlic until onion is soft. Sprinkle with flour and curry, cook and stir 3 minutes and gradually add milk. Cook and stir until thickened. Add rosemary, oregano and eggplant. Simmer 15 minutes. Puree in blender, add cream, reheat and serve.

CREAM OF ASPARAGUS SOUP

1 pound fresh asparagus
5 cups chicken stock
salt
4 tablespoons butter
4 tablespoons flour
¾ cup heavy cream
freshly ground white pepper
3 egg yolks
dash of lemon juice

Clean the asparagus, cutting off the woody ends and tips. Reserve the tips. Place the stock and asparagus in a heavy pan and cook for 40 to 50 minutes, covered. While the soup is simmering, drop asparagus tips into boiling water and cook for 3 to 5 minutes. Drain and reserve. Puree the stock and asparagus stalks in blender. Keep warm. Melt the butter and add the flour, cook for 2 minutes without browning. Add the pureed soup and bring to boil. Cook over low heat until slightly thick. Add 2 tablespoons cream and asparagus tips to soup. Just before serving, mix the remaining cream with egg yolks, whisk and add to soup with a dash of lemon juice. Reheat and serve.

VARIATION FOR CURRY LOVERS

Add about 2 teaspoons of powdered curry at the time you are adding the cream and asparagus tips.

SCOTCH KALE SOUP

5 cups beef stock
1½ cups kale, chopped
2 tablespoons rolled oats

Combine and simmer until the rolled oats are soft, about 30 minutes. Season with salt and pepper.

GREEN PEPPER SOUP

2 cups green pepper, minced
1 cup onion, minced
1 garlic clove, minced
3 slices bacon, minced
¼ cup carrot, minced
2 cups canned tomatoes
½ teaspoon salt
¼ teaspoon freshly ground black pepper
¼ teaspoon basil
4 cups beef stock
1 pound lean ground beef

Saute green pepper, onion, garlic, bacon and carrot until bacon is lightly browned. Add tomatoes, salt, pepper, basil, stock and meat. Cover, bring to a boil. Reduce heat and simmer for 45 minutes.

STUFFED PEPPER SOUP

½ cup white rice
3 pounds ripe unpeeled tomatoes, chopped
½ onion, finely minced
6 tablespoons cooking oil
¾ pound ground meat
large pinch oregano
freshly ground black pepper
1 garlic clove, mashed

6 - 8 green peppers, cleaned with tops removed
4 tablespoons flour
2 tablespoons tomato paste
3 cups water
bouquet garni
1 tablespoon sugar
1 teaspoon salt
2 small dried hot chili peppers

In a small saucepan bring 1½ cups of water to a boil. Add a pinch of salt and the rice and simmer over low heat, without stirring, for 20 minutes. Cool the rice and reserve. Puree tomatoes in blender. Heat 1 tablespoon oil. Add the onion and cook until soft but not browned. Combine the ground meat, onions, salt, oregano, pepper, cooked rice and garlic in a bowl. Correct the seasoning, then fill the peppers with the mixture. In a large pan, heat the remaining oil. Add the flour. Cook, stirring, until light brown. Add the tomato puree, tomato paste, 3 cups water and bouquet garni. Stir well to blend the flour and bring to a boil. Add the sugar, chili peppers, salt and pepper. Reduce the heat. Carefully place the stuffed peppers and meatballs in the soup. Cover and simmer over low heat for 1½ hours to 2 hours.

MENTON SOUP

1 pound fresh ripe tomatoes, peeled and chopped
2 cups new potatoes, cubed
2 onions, chopped
2 cups green beans, diced
3 small zucchini, cubed
½ cup spaghetti, broken-up
salt and freshly ground white pepper
1 cup fresh basil leaves
4 garlic cloves, minced
3 tablespoons freshly grated parmesan cheese
8 tablespoons olive oil

In a heavy pot heat 3 tablespoons olive oil. Add the onions and cook without browning for 3 to 5 minutes. Add the tomatoes, potatoes and beans. Season with salt and pepper and cover with 6 to 8 cups water. Bring the mixture to a boil and reduce the heat. Simmer the soup, partially covered, for 15 minutes. Add zucchini and spaghetti and continue simmering 12 to 15 minutes or until all the vegetables are tender. Don't overcook. While the soup is simmering, combine the basil, garlic and Parmesan in the top part of a double boiler. Add enough olive oil to make a smooth paste (about 5 tablespoons). Just before serving, whisk the basil paste into the soup.

ARTICHOKE SOUP

½ cup chopped onions
1 garlic clove, minced
1 tablespoon oil
4 artichokes
3 cups chicken stock
1 tablespoon lemon juice
½ tablespoon oregano
½ tablespoon black pepper

2 tablespoons green onions
(white part only), chopped
1 garlic clove, minced
1 tablespoon butter
2 cups half-and-half or
1 cup heavy cream
salt to taste
½ cup white wine

Saute garlic and onions in oil in a heavy pan. Add the artichokes, stock, lemon juice, oregano and pepper and simmer, covered, until artichokes are very tender (about 40 minutes). Remove artichokes, strain and reserve the stock. Scrape edible portion from the artrichoke leaves, remove chokes, dice hearts, reserving one heart for garnish. Saute green onions and garlic in butter until barely tender, puree in blender with artichokes and ½ cup of the reserved stock. Blend cream into puree, season with salt and pepper and reheat. Before serving, add the wine and diced artichoke heart.

BASIL SOUP

8 cups chicken stock
1 cup spaghetti, broken-up
2 small zucchini, diced
1 cup fresh basil leaves
1 tablespoon pine or hazel nuts
3 tablespoons grated Parmesan or Romano cheese
2 tablespoons oil
salt and pepper to taste

In large pot, bring stock to boil and add spaghetti. Cook about 9 minutes covered. Add zucchini, cover and cook for an additional 10 minutes. Place basil leaves, nuts, cheeses and oil in blender and puree. Whisk paste into stock mixture and serve.

CAULIFLOWER SOUP

4 cups cauliflowerets
4 cups chicken stock
1 teaspoon soy sauce
½ teaspoon each, savory, paprika and garlic powder
¼ teaspoon black pepper
2 tablespoons butter
2 tablespoons flour
1 cup cream
2 egg yolks, beaten
3 tablespoons lemon juice

Reserve ½ cup flowerets for garnish. Cook remainder in stock with soy sauce, savory, paprika, garlic powder and pepper until cauliflower is soft. Puree in blender. Melt butter until bubbly, add flour, cook and stir 3 minutes. Gradually add cream; cook and stir until thickened and add puree. Beat eggs with lemon juice, whisk in ½ cup hot soup and return to rest of soup. Reheat, but do not boil. Garnish with reserved cauliflowerets.

VARIATION FOR CHEESE LOVERS

Before adding eggs, add about ¼ cup freshly grated Parmesan or Romano cheese.

VIRGINIA PEANUT SOUP

2 stalks celery, chopped
1 small onion, chopped
4 tablespoons butter
2 tablespoons flour
1 cup crunchy peanut butter
4 cups chicken stock
2 teaspoons celery salt
1 tablespoon lemon juice
salt to taste
4 tablespoons coarsely chopped peanuts

Saute the onion and celery in butter until limp but not brown. Sprinkle with the flour and stir. Add the peanut butter. (Homemade peanut butter is really good in this—just put peanuts in blender, add enough butter to cream and chop.) Add the broth, celery salt, lemon juice and salt. Sprinkle the ground peanuts on the top of each bowl before serving.

COLD VEGETABLE SOUPS

BORSCHT

2 cups shredded fresh beets
1 cup chopped carrots
1 cup chopped onions
2⅔ cups salted water
1 quart beef stock
1 cup shredded cabbage
1 tablespoon lemon juice
6 tablespoons sour cream

Cook beets, carrots and onions uncovered in the salted water for 20 minutes. Add beef stock and shredded cabbage and cook uncovered 15 minutes longer. Puree in blender, add lemon juice, chill and serve in bowls, topping each with 1 tablespoon sour cream. (This is also delicious served hot.)

CARROT VICHYSSOISE

2 cups potatoes, peeled and diced
1¼ cups sliced carrots
1 leek, sliced (white part only)
3 cups chicken stock
salt
freshly ground white pepper
1 cup heavy cream

Place in saucepan: potatoes, carrots, leek and stock and bring to boil and simmer for 20 minutes. Puree half the vegetables at a time in blender for 30 seconds at high speed. Stir in white pepper, salt and cream. Chill. Serve garnished with shredded raw carrot.

CELERIAC SOUP

4 tablespoons butter
2 large onions, sliced
3 medium-sized potatoes, peeled and cubed
4 celery knobs, peeled and cubed
2 parsnips, peeled and cubed
salt and freshly ground white pepper
bouquet garni
8 cups chicken stock
1 cup heavy cream

Melt butter, add the onions and cook for 2 or 3 minutes, without browning. Add potatoes, celery cubes and parsnips. Season with salt and pepper and cover with chicken stock. Bring to boil and cook 45 minutes, partially covered. Uncover soup and cool. Puree in blender. Thin soup with cream. Sprinkle with parsley, chill and serve. (This is also marvelous served hot.)

COLD CUCUMBER SOUP

5 cucumbers
salt
½ cup chopped parsley
6 scallions, chopped
¼ cup lemon juice
2 tablespoons freshly chopped dill
1 quart buttermilk
1 pint sour cream
freshly ground white pepper

Peel the cucumbers, cut them in half lengthwise and remove the seeds. Sprinkle them with salt and let stand for 30 minutes. Drain off the accumulated water, chop the cucumbers coarsely and place them in blender with parsley, scallions, dill, lemon juice, buttermilk and sour cream. Blend at high speed. Add salt and pepper and chill. Garnish with finely diced cucumber or thinly sliced radishes.

GAZPACHO

There are as many *authentic* Gazpacho soup recipes as there are Democratic candidates for the Presidency (in other words, too numerous to count, too few worth remembering). Every province of Spain has at least one and every visitor to Spain brings back the only *true* version. We have scanned many for this book and selected only two—one cooked, one uncooked. We do not claim they are the *authentic* or *true* versions—only that they are good.

GAZPACHO I (Uncooked)

2 cups chicken stock	*1 red bell pepper*
2 cups bread crumbs	*2 garlic cloves*
3 pounds fresh tomatoes	*⅓ cup olive oil*
3 cucumbers	*2 teaspoons salt*
2 onions	*1 teaspoon chili powder*
1 green bell pepper	*¼ cup cider vinegar*

Place bread crumbs in stock and let stand for at least a half-hour. While crumbs are soaking, finely chop all vegetables. Add them to stock mixture, along with oil, seasonings and vinegar. Chill 3 hours. Serve garnished with sliced stuffed green olives, minced parsley and chopped celery. Also offer bowls of chopped vegetables to add to mixture.

GAZPACHO II (Cooked)

3 cups chicken stock
3 cups water
4 tomatoes, peeled and chopped
2 onions, diced
4 garlic cloves
1 cup green bell pepper, chopped
1 cucumber, peeled and chopped
4 tablespoons olive oil
½ cup celery, chopped
2 tablespoons fresh lemon juice
¼ teaspoon chili powder

Bring stock and water to boil. Add all other ingredients and simmer for 20 minutes. Cool and puree in blender. Chill for at least 3 hours before serving. Dice more onion, tomatoes, cucumber, bell pepper and several ripe avocados and place in separate bowls. You might want to fill another bowl with grated cheddar cheese. Fill another bowl with croutons and serve with the Gazpacho. (The idea is that guests will add whatever they want to the basic soup.)

GREEN BEAN PUREE

2 cups each, lamb and pork stock
1 pound green beans, cut up
½ cup sour cream
1½ cup half-and-half
1 teaspoon lemon juice
½ teaspoon salt
¼ teaspoon white pepper
⅛ teaspoon savory

Cook beans in stock until tender. Puree in blender and cool. Beat sour cream with a little half-and-half, combine with beans and season with lemon juice, salt, pepper and savory. Chill, adjust seasonings and serve garnished with lemon slices and parsley.

ICED PARSLEY AND TARRAGON

1 large bunch parsley
2 tablespoons butter
2 large leeks, finely sliced
1 pound new potatoes, peeled and cubed
6 cups chicken stock
salt and freshly ground white pepper
2 cups light cream
2 tablespoons fresh tarragon, finely chopped

Wash the parsley. Remove the coarse stems. Chop the leaves. This should yield about 3 cups. Reserve 2 tablespoons for garnishing. In a heavy pan, melt the butter, add leeks and cook over moderate heat until soft but not browned. Add the potato cubes and chicken stock. Bring to a boil. Season with salt and pepper. Reduce heat, cover and simmer until the potatoes are soft (about 35 minutes). Add the chopped parsley and simmer for 10 minutes. Puree the soup in blender. Add the cream and tarragon. Chill until ready to serve. Garnish with remaining parsley and sliced radishes.

VICHYSSOISE

4 leeks, cleaned
1 medium sized onion, peeled and sliced thin
4 tablespoons butter
6 medium-sized potatoes, peeled and sliced thin
1 quart chicken stock
2 cups milk
2 cups light cream
¾ teaspoon salt
1 cup heavy cream
¾ cup chopped chives

Slice white part of the leeks, lightly brown with onion in butter, then add potatoes. Add stock. Boil 35 minutes. Puree in blender. Add milk, light cream and salt and bring to boil. Cool and add heavy cream. Serve cold garnished with chives.

COLD ZUCCHINI SOUP

6 small zucchini, cut into 1 inch cubes,
(save a few slices for garnish)
2 tablespoons oil
2 tablespoons butter
salt
2 onions, finely chopped
5 cups chicken stock
1 - 2 teaspoons lemon juice
freshly ground pepper
bouquet garni

Salt the zucchini cubes and place them in sieve over a bowl for at least 30 minutes to drain. In a large casserole, heat the olive oil and butter. Add the onion and garlic and cook over low heat without browning, for about 5 minutes. Dry the zucchini cubes and add them to the skillet and continue cooking over low heat for 5 minutes. Add the chicken stock and bouquet garni and let the soup simmer for 15 minutes. Remove garni, cool and puree in blender. Add the herbs and lemon juice. Season with salt and pepper and chill. Garnish the soup with sour cream mixed with chives or grated raw zucchini. If it gets too thick, thin out with heavy cream or milk.

•   **NOTES**   •

POTAGE VERT PRE

3 tablespoons butter
½ cup minced scallions
3 tablespoons flour
4 cups fresh tiny peas
1 cup fresh spinach leaves
1 head Boston lettuce, shredded
1 tablespoon sugar
6 cups chicken stock
salt
1 cup heavy cream
3 egg yolks
freshly ground white pepper

Melt the butter over medium heat, add scallions and cook until tender without browning. Add the flour, cook over low heat for 2 or 3 minutes. Add 3 cups of the peas, spinach, lettuce and sugar. Cover with the chicken stock and bring to a boil. Reduce heat, cover and simmer for 45 minutes. Cover the remaining peas with water in a small saucepan and cook until barely tender. Drain and reserve. Puree the soup in a blender and return to pot over low heat. Mix the cream and egg yolks and whisk into the soup. Add the whole peas, pepper and serve. (This is also delicious served hot).

•   **NOTES**   •

six

BEEF, LAMB AND PORK SOUPS

We were sitting in a San Francisco pub recently, enjoying a little libation during a break in a business conference when we were joined by a young man we hadn't seen in some time. After the usual opening pleasantries, we got on to some fairly serious matters, including his brother's rocky marital problems. He then informed us that he had, himself, gone to the altar since we last met and we jokingly asked if he thought his marriage would last. "I'm sure it will," he said, "mainly because my wife *lies* a lot." We were both stunned by that reply, but passed it off, figuring it was essentially his business. We were both wondering, however, if this wasn't one of those *modern* marriages we read about and couldn't help but silently ask: Lies about what? Fidelity? Her past? Her future plans? Her feelings about him? What? we wanted to shriek. Well, after about a half-hour of this kind of agonizing going on inside while trying to enjoy the continuing conversation outside, it came out that his wife was a stewardess. What he had said was she *flies* a lot, meaning she was out of town a good deal of the time and that they both believed in that old standard that absence makes the heart grow fonder. That's why he figured the marriage would work.

Confusing, eh? Well, if you want confusion, try writing a cookbook, particularly a soup cookbook. We both shouldn't be a bit surprised to discover that there are many certifiably insane librarians running around, especially if they've been involved in categorizing things. As we pointed out in the introduction to chicken soups, many fruit soups have chicken stock bases. Does that make them chicken soups? Does cold lemon soup become "chicken with lemons" because it has a chicken stock base? Or does chicken become "cold lemon with chicken" for the same reason? (These questions, to be effective, must be asked in Gene Wilder's patented demonstration of controlled, but growing, hysteria.)

We have done our best to sort out these problems throughout the book without professional medical help, but must throw up our hands when we get into this section. Some recipes herein call for equal portions of beef, lamb and pork. Others have pork in chicken stock while still others call for lamb in a combination of chicken and pork stocks. Just recalling them sends us roaming about the house chanting "Porkin and Chork," "Lamkin and Chickamb" and other absurd things. So, friends, they have become arbitrary. Remember, though, when you get into the area of beef, lamb and pork, they are almost always interchangeable.

Just mix 'em or match 'em!

BEEF SOUPS

BEEF 'N' BEER SOUP

2 pounds stewing beef, cubed
3 tablespoons butter
4 onions, chopped
5 cups beef stock
bouquet garni
1 bottle (12 ounces) dark beer
1 tablespoon brown sugar
1 tablespoon vinegar

Heat butter in large saucepan and brown meat. Remove and set aside. Add onions and stir-fry until transparent. Pour over stock and add garni and brown sugar. Simmer, covered, until beef is almost done (about 35 minutes). Add beer and simmer an additional 10 minutes. Remove garni, swirl in vinegar and serve garnished with freshly grated cheese or grated carrots.

BEEF STRACCIATELLA

3 pounds stewing meat, cubed
3 tablespoons butter
bouquet garni
8 cups beef stock
1½ cups uncooked vermicelli or other thin pasta
2 eggs
1½ teaspoon semolina
3 tablespoons grated Romano or Parmesan cheese
salt and pepper to taste

Melt butter in heavy saucepan and brown meat chunks. Heat stock to boiling point, add garni and beef. Simmer, covered, until beef is almost done (about 30 minutes). Remove garni, add pasta and cook until done. Remove from heat and take out 1 cup of the stock. Set aside to cool. When cool, combine with eggs, semolina and cheese and mix well. Slowly stir into stock mixture, reheat and serve.

VARIATIONS

1. Add 1½ cups cooked, diced green beans to soup before adding egg mixture.
2. Add 1½ cups cooked peas to soup before adding egg mixture.

VEAL STRACCIATELLA

Substitute 3 pounds veal chunks for beef and use even mixture of chicken and veal stock.

PORK STRACCIATELLA

Substitute 3 pounds chunks of cooked pork roast for beef and use even mixture of pork and beef stock.

BEEF GUMBO WITH RICE

2 pounds stewing beef, cubed
3 tablespoons butter
8 cups beef stock and 2 cups water
1 cup fresh tomatoes, peeled and pureed
1 onion, chopped
½ red pepper, diced
3 green peppers, diced
salt and pepper to taste
1 quart fresh okra, sliced
½ pound cooked ham, diced
6 cups rice, cooked

Brown beef in heavy saucepan with butter. Stir in stock, tomato puree, onion and peppers. Simmer, covered, until meat is tender (about 45 minutes). Add salt, pepper, okra and ham and cook an additional 5 minutes; add rice and cook an additional 2 minutes.

CARROT-BEEF SOUP

1 pound stewing beef, cubed
3 tablespoons butter
1 onion, chopped
6 large carrots, peeled and thinly sliced
8 cups beef stock
3 tablespoons parsley, minced

Melt butter in heavy saucepan. Brown meat and remove. Add onions and carrots and stir-fry over low heat until onions are transparent. Add meat and pour over beef stock. Add parsley, bring to boil and simmer until meat is tender (about 45 minutes). Garnish with freshly grated carrots and parsley.

HAMBURGER SOUP

2 pounds ground beef
1 pound fresh mushrooms, sliced
3 tablespoons butter
2 cups carrots, grated
1½ cups onions, chopped
½ cups green pepper, diced
8 cups beef stock
bouquet garni
2 tomatoes, peeled and diced
1 pound red kidney beans, cooked and drained

Melt butter in heavy saucepan and add mushrooms. Gently saute until done. Remove with slotted spoon and set aside. Add carrots, onions and green pepper and stir-fry until onions are transparent. Add ground beef and stir-fry until done. Pour over stock, add garni and tomatoes and simmer, covered, for about 45 minutes. Add beans and simmer an additional 15 minutes. Serve garnished with grated cheddar cheese.

MEATBALL SOUP

8 cups beef stock
2 pounds ground beef
½ cup cracker crumbs
3 eggs
½ teaspoon marjoram
½ teaspoon basil
½ teaspoon rosemary
½ teaspoon thyme
4 carrots, thinly chopped
1 cup fresh peas, cooked and drained
2 green onions, chopped fine
4 tablespoons vin rose

Heat stock to boiling and while that's being done, combine meat, cracker crumbs, eggs, salt and pepper to taste, and herbs in a separate bowl. Mix well and form into ½ inch balls. Add carrots, peas and onion to stock and simmer about 10 minutes. Add meatballs one at a time and simmer until meat is done (about 5 minutes). Swirl in wine and serve garnished with grated cheese or grated carrots.

OX TAIL SOUP

1 ox tail, cut into 2 inch sections
6 tablespoons flour
6 tablespoons butter
10 cups beef stock
½ cup carrots, diced
1 onion, chopped
½ cup celery, diced
1 teaspoon brandy
⅓ cup sherry
1 teaspoon lemon rind, grated

Heat butter in large, heavy saucepan and brown tail sections after dredging in flour (about 10 minutes). Add stock and simmer, covered, for 2 hours. Add carrot, onion and celery and simmer an additional hour. Swirl in brandy, sherry and lemon rind and serve garnished with fresh parsley or grated carrots.

LAMB SOUPS

ALBONDIGAS SOUP

½ pound ground pork
½ pound ground lamb
1 pound lean ground beef
1 slice bread
milk
2 eggs, beaten slightly
½ teaspoon pepper
2 teaspoons salt
8 - 10 pimento stuffed olives
1 tablespoon chili powder
1 onion, chopped
2 tablespoons butter
2 cloves garlic, minced
3 medium tomatoes, peeled and mashed
2 cups beef stock
¼ teaspoon oregano

(continued)

Mix the meats and soak the bread in milk and squeeze dry. Blend with meats, eggs and seasonings. Shape into meatballs about the size of a walnut with an olive half in the middle of each. Set aside. Heat the butter and saute the garlic and onion until golden. Add the tomatoes and oregano. Stir in the stock. Bring to a boil, add meatballs and reduce heat. Cover and simmer for 1 hour.

ITALIAN LAMB SOUP

10 cups lamb stock
7 egg yolks
3 teaspoons fresh lemon juice
⅓ teaspoon marjoram, crushed
salt and pepper to taste

In a large, heavy saucepan, beat eggs thoroughly with a fork. Add lemon juice and about ½ teaspoon salt and continue beating a few minutes. In a separate pot, bring stock to boil and pour slowly over egg mixture, stirring constantly. Cook very slowly about 5 minutes or until thickened. Serve in bowls over toasted French bread or garlic croutons and garnish with freshly grated Romano or Parmesan cheese.

MULLIGATAWNY SOUP

1 onion
1 carrot
1 small white turnip
4 tablespoons butter
1 pound lamb
1 teaspoon curry powder
6 cups chicken stock
bouquet garni
1 apple, peeled, cored and cut into pieces
1 teaspoon lemon juice
1 cup cooked rice

Slice the onion thinly, cut the carrot and turnip, saute in butter. When brown, add lamb to pot and sear. Add curry powder. Cook for 5 minutes, stirring. Add hot chicken stock. Bring to boil, skim and cook for 2 hours. Strain, put lamb pieces back in soup and bring to boil again. Add apple and lemon juice and simmer for 5 minutes. Add rice, heat through and serve.

PHILADELPHIA HOT POT

1 pound honeycomb tripe, washed, drained and cut up
3 tablespoons butter
1 pound stewing lamb, cut up
¼ pound lean salt pork
1 clove
bouquet garni
3 cups cold water
1 pint mixed vegetables
½ pint diced potatoes
salt and pepper to taste
⅓ cup flour
⅓ cup butter
2 egg yolks, beaten

Whatever vegetables are in season may be used in this recipe. Saute tripe in 3 tablespoons butter until golden brown. Add the lamb, salt pork, seasonings and bouquet garni with the cold water. Cover and bring to boil and simmer 2 hours. Add the vegetables and simmer for 20 minutes. After cooling, remove fat, season to taste and thicken with flour and butter creamed together. Add egg yolks and serve.

PORK SOUPS

CHINESE PORK AND CELERY CABBAGE SOUP

2½ pounds pork chops, after boned and defatted
3 tablespoons oil
1½ tablespoons soy sauce
¾ teaspoon cornstarch
8 cups pork stock or equal mixture of pork and chicken stock
1 teaspoon honey
salt and pepper to taste
1 pound celery cabbage

Heat oil in heavy saucepan and cook chops, covered, until done. Dice meat. Mix soy sauce and cornstarch until smooth and add meat to it. Heat stock and add honey, salt and pepper and all the cabbage after it has been shredded. Simmer about 30 minutes, add marinated pork and sauce and stir well. Simmer an additional 10 minutes and serve garnished with a little grated ginger root.

HOT ITALIAN SAUSAGE SOUP

10 cups chicken stock,
(or combination of chicken and pork stock)
½ pound dried white pea beans, cooked
3 tablespoons oil
5 hot Italian sausages (about 4 inches in length)
2 onions, chopped
2 celery stalks, chopped
5 tomatoes, peeled and diced
4 potatoes, peeled and diced
2 carrots
salt and pepper to taste
bouquet garni

Soak the beans in water for about 3 hours, then drain. Pour over stock and simmer until beans are almost done (about 1½ hours). Set aside. In a large, heavy saucepan, heat the oil and brown sliced sausage. Stir in tomatoes, potatoes, carrots, onions, celery and salt and pepper. Simmer for about 20 minutes, add garni and pour over the beans and stock. Simmer an additional half hour. Remove garni and serve garnished with freshly grated Romano or Parmesan cheese.

PORK HEART SOUP

2 pounds pork heart (or cubed, cooked pork)
⅛ pound pork rind, diced
3 tablespoons oil
1 cup dry red wine
4 tablespoons tomato paste
bouquet garni
½ teaspoon rosemary
4 cup pork stock
4 cups beef stock

Heat oil in heavy saucepan and brown pork meat and rind over high heat. Add salt and pepper to taste and the wine. Mix tomato paste in a little warm water and add it to pan along with garni and rosemary. Pour over the combined stocks and simmer gently for about 2 hours. Remove garni and serve over croutons, garnished with grated Parmesan or Romano cheese.

POSOLE DE CHICOS

We have some friends who have made soup a traditional serving at their annual New Year's Eve party. People bring their favorites and this one has become everyone's favorite as the years have gone by. Chicos are kernels of green corn cut from the cob after being steamed and dried. Hominy may be substituted, but the soup suffers.

2 cups chicos
6 cups water
1 pound pork ribs
⅓ pound pork rind
4 red chili pods, dried
2 teaspoons salt
2 cloves garlic, chopped
2 teaspoons oregano
2 teaspoons saffron

Heat water in a heavy pot and add chicos. Cook until kernels begin to burst. Then add meat and chili and simmer at least 2 hours or until meat is thoroughly cooked. Add salt, garlic, oregano and saffron and simmer an additional 30 minutes. Serve with hot buttered flour tortillas.

SCOTTIE'S SAUSAGE-BEAN CHOWDER

1 pound sausage
2 #10 cans kidney beans
1 large can tomatoes, crushed
1 quart water or stock
1 large onion, chopped
1 bay leaf
1½ teaspoon salt
½ teaspoon thyme
⅛ teaspoon pepper
1 cup elbow macaroni
½ cup green pepper, chopped
Parmesan cheese

In a skillet, cook sausage until brown. Pour off fat. In a large kettle, combine beans, tomatoes, liquid, onion, seasonings. Add meat, simmer covered for 1 hour. Add macaroni and green pepper and cook, covered, for another 15 or 20 minutes. Sprinkle with Parmesan and serve.

SPARERIB MINESTRONE

2½ quarts water
1 pound spareribs, separated
½ pound sweet Italian sausage
3 onions, chopped
4 white turnips, chopped
3 stalks celery, chopped
½ medium cabbage, shredded
½ chicory head, shredded
5 stalks Swiss chard, shredded
salt and pepper to taste
bouquet garni

Mix all vegetables together and divide in half. Place half in large soup pot and cover with spareribs and sausage. Cover with remaining vegetables, add garni, cover and simmer for about 3 hours. Remove from heat and allow to cool. Remove garni. Skim scum from top, reheat and serve garnished with garlic croutons and grated Parmesan or Romano cheese.

SOPA POBLANO

1 tablespoon oil
¼ pound lean pork, cut into small cubes
½ medium onion, chopped
kernels from 1 fresh ear of corn
3 tablespoons tomato puree
1 small zucchini, thinly sliced
1 chili poblano, thinly sliced
1 quart chicken stock
1 ripe avocado, peeled, seeded and diced
¼ cup grated Parmesan cheese

Saute the pork in 1 tablespoon oil over medium heat, until brown. Add onion, corn, poblano, zucchini, tomato puree and stock and simmer until vegetables are tender, about 20 minutes. Just before serving, add salt to taste and avocado, and grated cheese.

WATERCRESS AND PORKBALL SOUP

1 tablespoon finely chopped fresh ginger
1 pound finely ground pork
2 scallions, finely chopped
8 - 10 water chestnuts, finely chopped
1 teaspoon salt
1½ teaspoons soy sauce
¼ teaspoon freshly ground white pepper
2 teaspoons cornstarch
10 cups pork or chicken stock
4 ounces thin Chinese noodles
2 bunches watercress

Combine ginger, pork, scallions, water chestnuts, salt, soy sauce, pepper and cornstarch. Mix and form into balls. Makes about 55 meatballs. Soak noodles in hot water until soft, about 30 minutes. Bring the stock to a boil and poach a few meatballs at a time until they float. Remove and set aside. Wash and drain watercress, removing any tough stems. Just before serving, bring stock to a boil and add noodles. Cook about 2 minutes. Season with salt and pepper. Add watercress and cook, uncovered, just until the watercress is wilted and bright green.

•   **NOTES**   •

seven

POULTRY SOUPS

In the whole world there are two reasons and two reasons only for raising or having anything else physically to do with chickens. One is to *make* money and the other is to *save* money. Even the most ardent vegetarian could not like, let alone love, chickens. They are dirty and brainless; noisy and unmanageable. They lure to your property such varmints as coyotes and snakes and if they don't kill one another off, some mysterious disease will. Frankly, lizards have more endearing qualities. But, Lord, chickens do lay eggs—and they do make for incredible soups.

If Betty MacDonald had not written *The Egg and I*, our good friends Bob and Gayle Allen surely would have. Bob and Gayle are egg freaks, proven out by the fact that they have somehow been able to compile an entire book of egg recipes (entitled, for some reason, *The Egg Book*, Celestial Arts, 1975). In addition to being a writer, Bob is a photographer, film-maker, sometimes actor, world-traveler and for the past several years, the accidental proprietor of a mini-chicken ranch (the ranch is mini, not the chickens). Bob was photographing an Easter layout for a magazine and purchased a gaggle of cuddly yellow chicks to romp across the cover. Afterwards, of course, they were still there so Bob, visions of fresh eggs dancing in his head, constructed a coop. It only took a couple of weekends and lots of wood (read that gold), wire, toil, sweat, tears and heating devices. There is a period of time between the cuddly chick period and the ugly, but egg-laying period and it took the Allens quite a bit of work to keep the dozen new members of their family healthy. Some got sick anyway and, in spite of personal nursing care, passed on. By the end of the year, two were left and Bob took to dark mumblings when the subject came up. Finally, however, an egg appeared in the coop, then another, and now the Allens harvest at least one a day. We figure that at the present rate they will have recovered all the money and time spent around the turn of the century and we know, even though Bob won't admit it, that he wishes he had used a gun instead of a camera for the original shooting.

Now, to the good news: Chicken Soup. Golden, rich, nutritious, delicious chicken soup. Chicken soup with vegetables, with noodles, with rice, and macaroni, by itself, with cream, with matzo balls, with split peas, with just about anything your heart or palate desires. It is *the* soup and its many uses made it a little difficult for us to categorize many of the recipes in this book because so many of the vegetable and even fruit soups use chicken stock as a base. So, what we have done is to list in this chapter those dishes in which chicken *and* chicken stock are main ingredients (except the matzo ball soup). At the end of the chapter, you will also find a little something for the turkey and duck fanciers.

CREAM OF CHICKEN SOUP
(Basic Recipe)

8 cups chicken stock
2 cups heavy cream
7 tablespoons butter
7 tablespoons flour
salt and pepper to taste

Melt butter in heavy saucepan and slowly add flour, stirring constantly. Cook, still stirring constantly, until paste is thick and slightly brown (about 3 minutes). Slowly add hot stock, again stirring all the while. Simmer about 20 minutes. In separate pan, heat but do not boil, the cream. Slowly stir into soup and serve. Garnish with finely grated carrots.

VARIATIONS

1. Add 2 cups diced cooked chicken about 5 minutes before adding cream.
2. Add 1 cup sauteed sliced mushrooms just before adding cream.
3. Add 2 cups cooked green peas about 2 minutes before adding cream.
4. Add 1½ cups cooked and chunked asparagus tips about 2 minutes before adding cream.
5. Add 2 cups cooked and drained egg noodles about 3 minutes before adding cream.
6. Add 2 cups diced artichoke hearts about 3 minutes before adding cream.
7. Add 1½ cups cooked and diced ham or shellfish.
8. Add any or all of the variations 1 through 7 along with an additional 2 cups chicken stock and 1½ cups cooked and diced potatoes and you have a marvelous cream of chicken stew—truly a meal in itself!

CREAM OF CHICKEN WITH VEGETABLES

3 pounds whole chicken, cut up
5 cups chicken stock
2 cups beef stock
3 tablespoons butter
3 onions, chopped
1 carrot, chopped
1 celery stalk, chopped
bouquet garni with peppercorns and cloves added
2 cups heavy cream
3 egg yolks
⅓ cup cooked peas
⅓ cup cooked corn
¼ cup sauteed sliced mushrooms

In heavy saucepan, melt butter and add chopped onions, carrot and celery. Stir-fry over low heat until onions are transparent. Put in blender with about a cup of the stock and blend until smooth. Pour stock in pot, stir in pureed vegetables mixture and add chicken, salt and pepper and bouquet garni. Bring to boil and simmer, partially covered, until chicken is done (about 1 hour). Remove chicken and garni. Cool soup and skim any scum from the top. When chicken cools, skin and dice the white meat (save the dark meat for chicken salad sandwiches or chicken salad). Reheat soup and beat egg yolks and cream. Remove about 2 cups of the hot stock and stir it into yolk-cream mixture. Slowly stir back into soup. Add peas, corn, mushrooms and diced meat. Reheat for about 5 minutes, being careful not to boil. Garnish with grated carrots or fresh-grated Parmesan or Romano cheese.

AUSTRIAN CREAM OF CHICKEN SOUP

8 cups chicken stock
3 chicken livers
6 tablespoons butter
½ pound mushrooms, sliced
2 teaspoons fresh lemon juice
salt and pepper to taste
1½ cups small fresh peas
½ cup water
4 tablespoons flour
2 egg yolks
1 cup heavy cream
bouquet garni

In a heavy pan, melt half of the butter and stir-fry diced chicken livers until done. Remove with slotted spoon and reserve. In separate pan, cook mushrooms, lemon juice and salt and pepper for 5 minutes over low heat. Set aside to cool. In still another pan, cook peas in water until done. Drain and reserve. Heat stock and while it is heating, melt remaining butter in pan and slowly add flour. Stir-fry until thick brown paste emerges (about 5 minutes). Add a little stock, stir and then stir into remaining stock. Add mushrooms, peas and liver to stock. Mix egg yolks and cream, add slowly to stock and serve. Garnish with grated cheese or grated carrots.

LOU'S CHICKEN AND MACARONI SOUP

1 quart chicken stock
5 chicken legs and thighs, split
1 celery stalk, chopped
1 carrot, coarsely grated
6 green onions, chopped
¼ cup vin rose
½ cup Romano cheese, grated
1½ cup uncooked macaroni
bouquet garni
salt and pepper to taste

Cover chicken with stock, bring to boil and skim. Add celery, carrot, green onion, wine and bouquet garni. Simmer, covered, until chicken is done (about 1½ hours). Remove chicken and cool. Skim pot, add cheese and simmer about 30 minutes, very slowly. Add macaroni and cook until done. Skin cooled chicken and dice the meat. Add to pot, heat and serve.

VARIATIONS

Chicken Noodle Soup. Substitute egg noodles for macaroni. You may also want to omit the cheese.

Chicken Rice Soup. Substitute rice for macaroni. Again, you may also want to omit the cheese.

CURRIED CHICKEN AND GREEN PEA SOUP

1 onion, finely chopped
1 clove garlic
2 tablespoons oil
1 tablespoon butter
2 cups shelled fresh peas
2 teaspoons curry powder
2 tablespoons flour
2 cups chicken stock
1 cup finely chopped cooked chicken meat
1 cup light cream
salt and freshly ground pepper

Heat the butter and vegetables oil in saucepan. Add the onion and garlic and cook slowly for 5 minutes. Add the peas, reduce heat and simmer slowly until peas are soft. Add curry powder, cook another minute. Remove from heat and add flour. Add the chicken stock and return to heat. Cook, stirring constantly, until soup boils. Remove from heat and puree in blender. Return to pan, add chicken meat, cream, salt and pepper. If served cold, thin with a little milk.

8 cups chicken stock
1¾ cups diced cooked white meat of chicken
¾ cups mushrooms, finely diced
½ cup green onions, finely chopped
¼ teaspoon cayenne pepper
¼ teaspoon salt
1 teaspoon fresh lemon juice
⅓ teaspoon oregano
½ pound broken vermicilli or other pasta
3 eggs
1 cup heavy cream
8 tablespoons grated Romano or Parmesan cheese
bouquet garni
salt and pepper to taste
2 tablespoons oil

In large, heavy pot, heat oil and add mushrooms, onion, cayenne, salt, lemon juice and oregano. Stir-fry over low heat until mushrooms are tender. Add stock, bring to boil and stir in pasta. Cook until pasta is done (about 8 minutes). Beat eggs and cream in bowl. Whisk in about a cup of the stock, mix well and slowly return to soup. Remove garni, add cheese and chicken, garnish with paprika and parsley and serve.

CHICKEN AND CLAM SOUP WITH ROYALES

7 cups chicken stock
1 cup clam juice
salt and pepper to taste
Royales (see recipe below)

Heat combined stock and clam juice. Add seasonings and let simmer for a few minutes. Divide Royales equally and place one in each bowl, sprinkle with about a teaspoon of sherry. Ladle on the stock and garnish with minced chives and dashes of paprika.

ROYALES

½ cup stock
1 garlic clove, minced
2 sprigs fresh parsley
⅛ teaspoon savory
⅛ teaspoon paprika
1 egg yolk

Place stock, garlic, parsley, savory and paprika in heavy saucepan and simmer for about 12 minutes. Puree in blender until smooth. Cool, then beat in egg yolk. Pour into buttered baking pan and bake at 250° until knife inserted in center comes out clean (about 30 minutes). Cool and then cut into individual servings.

QUICK CHICKEN LIVER-CELERY SOUP

½ pound chicken livers
¼ cup vegetable oil
½ cup celery, diced
1 quart milk
¾ cup flour
½ teaspoon savory
salt and pepper to taste

Clean, dice and gently cook liver in oil until done. Slowly add all other ingredients to blender and blend until smooth. Add livers last and blend for just a few moments longer (or until completely pureed, if you prefer it that way). Heat gently, being careful not to boil, and serve garnished with fresh lemon slices and paprika.

TORTELLINI

8 cups chicken broth
3 eggs
1½ cups flour
¼ pound chicken, cooked and diced
⅛ pound roast pork, cooked and diced
2 slices prosciutto, chopped
⅛ teaspoon grated parmesan or Romano cheese
⅛ teaspoon nutmeg
salt and pepper to taste

Heat chicken broth and while it's heating, mix 2 of the eggs with the flour, kneading for about 15 minutes. Roll very thin and cut in 3 inch circles. In a separate bowl, mix all other ingredients well. Stuff each dough piece with about a teaspoon of the mixture and pinch closed with fingers. (Each tortellini should have the appearance of a little dunce cap.) Bring stock to boil and drop tortellinis in one by one. Simmer about 20 minutes and serve garnished with parsley leaves.

MATZO BALL SOUP

1 quart chicken stock
2 eggs
2 tablespoons vegetable oil
½ cup matzo meal
salt to taste
pinch of nutmeg

Beat eggs well and mix in the oil. Add matzo meal, salt and nutmeg and mix well. Chill for at least 30 minutes. Bring stock to boil and let simmer uncovered while you form matzo balls. Have a bowl of water nearby and keep hands moist as you form the one-inch balls. Drop one ball in stock and cook about 15 minutes to make sure they will hold form. Add others one at a time and cook for about 30 minutes.

VARIATIONS

1. Form balls around finely chopped liver.
2. Substitute ½ teaspoon almond extract for nutmeg.
3. Substitute 1 teaspoon ginger for nutmeg.
4. Substitute 2 tablespoons parsley for nutmeg.
5. Substitute 1 tablespoon finely chopped nuts for nutmeg.
6. Stuff each ball with ½ blanched almond.

DUCK SOUP

4 cups chicken stock
4 cups duck stock (follow recipe for chicken stock, using
leftover duck meat and carcass instead of chicken)
1 ½ cup duck meat, diced
1 celery stalk, chopped
1 carrot, coarsley grated
6 green onions
¼ cup vin rose
½ cup Romano cheese, grated
bouquet garni
salt and pepper to taste
1 tablespoon finely grated orange rind

Bring stock mixture to boil, add celery, carrot, onion, wine and bouquet garni. Simmer, covered, about 45 minutes. Add cheese gradually, stirring constantly, and simmer very slowly for about 30 minutes. Remove garni, add orange rind and duck meat and simmer for 5 more minutes before serving.

VARIATIONS

Duck Noodle Soup. Before adding duck meat, add 1½ cups uncooked egg noodles. Simmer until done.

Duck Rice Soup. Substitute rice for noodles.

Quick Noodle or Rice Soup. Cook the noodles or rice first, then add a few minutes before serving.

CREAM OF TURKEY SOUP
(Basic Recipe)

8 cups turkey stock, (use basic chicken stock recipe,
substituting turkey for chicken)
2 cups heavy cream
7 tablespoons butter
7 tablespoons flour
salt and pepper to taste

Melt butter in heavy saucepan and slowly add flour, stirring constantly. Cook, still stirring constantly, until paste is thick and slightly brown (about 3 minutes). Slowly add hot stock, again stirring all the while. Simmer about 20 minutes. In separate pan, heat but do not boil the cream. Slowly stir into soup and serve. Garnish with finely grated carrots.

Variations

1. For slightly different taste, use 5 cups turkey stock and 3 cups beef stock.

2. Add 2 cups diced cooked turkey meat about 5 minutes before adding cream.

3. Add 1 cup sauteed sliced mushrooms just before adding cream.

4. Add 2 cups cooked green peas about 2 minutes before adding cream.

5. Add 1½ cups cooked and chunked asparagus tips about 2 minutes before adding cream.

6. Add 2 cups cooked and drained egg noodles about 3 minutes before adding cream.

7. Add 2 cups diced artichoke hearts about 3 minutes before adding cream.

8. Add 1½ cups cooked and diced ham or shellfish.

9. Add any or all of variations 1 through 8 along with an additional 2 cups stock and 1½ cups cooked and diced potatoes and you have a marvelous turkey stew—a meal in itself.

eight

GIFTS FROM THE SEA

With most cooking, there is a "point of no return," a juncture beyond which all is lost. When you discover the prime rib is overdone, for instance, there is no way of recovering the rareness. Or the point where the cake falls or when you discover, upon tasting, that the souffle needs a little more cheese. Or this problem faced by a barber of our acquaintance. He had just put the finishing touches on a customer, brushed him and spun him slowly around in the chair so that he could admire the work in the surrounding mirrors. "I'd like it a little bit longer in the back and quite a bit longer on the sides," he said, straight-faced. All of these woes come after the fact, beyond that point of no return. With soups, however, there is no such point. Corrections can always be made—right up to serving time. If you find your cheese soups needs more cheese, for instance, just grate some more and swirl it in. The same is true for mushrooms, vegetables . . . just about anything.

If there is an exception, it would be with some of the more delicate fish soups. You don't ever want to overcook the fish. Overcooked scallops, for example, take on the taste and texture of little rubber balls. It's not unlike playing golf on a busy course. When you've putted out, get off the green! When the fish is done, get it out of the pot! This way you can also prepare the soup hours ahead of time. Just reserve the fish and put it back in at the last minute before serving, cooking it just enough to heat it up.

ABALONE SOUP

1 pound abalone, cooked and diced
3 cups chicken stock
2 cups fish stock
2 cups fresh peas
bouquet garni

Heat stocks in pot and add garni. When liquid comes to boil, add peas and cook until almost done. Add abalone and continue cooking until peas are tender and abalone is hot.

BALKAN FISH SOUP

3 pints small fresh mussels
2 onions, sliced
bouquet garni
10 peppercorns
2 cups white wine
2 tablespoons butter
3 tablespoons flour
1 leek, sliced
1 celery stalk, sliced
1 carrot, sliced
5 cups water
2 pounds fish trimmings
2½ pounds bass or other firm white fish
salt and freshly ground white pepper
½ pound small raw, fresh shrimp, peeled
3 egg yolks
2 tablespoons lemon juice
½ cup heavy cream
1 tablespoon chopped parsley
2 tablespoons chopped fresh dill

Clean the mussels thoroughly under cold water, scrubbing well to remove all sand. Place them in a large kettle. Add the onions, bouquet garni, peppercorns and wine. Cover and bring to a boil, steaming the mussels for 5 to 10 minutes. Strain the mussel stock through cheesecloth and set aside. Remove the mussels from the shells and reserve. Melt the butter. Add the flour and cook for 2 minutes. Add the vegetables and cook for 5 minutes. Add the fish trimmings and mussel stock together with the water and let simmer for 45 minutes. Strain and return to the pot. Season the fish pieces with salt and pepper, add to the stock and simmer for 10 minutes or until the fish is flakey. Remove the fish pieces with a slotted spoon and put them in a serving tureen. Add the shrimp to the stock, cook 5 minutes. Put them in the tureen. Beat the egg yolks with lemon juice and cream. Gradually add a cup of the hot stock, whisking constantly. Return to soup. Heat but don't boil. Correct the seasoning and, if you like, add more lemon juice. Garnish with parsley and dill and lemon slices.

SIMPLE BOUILLABAISSE

5 pound mixture of lobster, crab and any fresh fillet of fish
you can lay your hands on
10 cups fish stock

While stock is being brought to boil, cut all the fish into small pieces and slowly add to stock. Cook over very hot fire until fish is done (certainly not more than 10 minutes). Serve over pieces of toasted French bread placed in each bowl and garnish with fresh parsley.

VARIATIONS

You could probably fill a book with the variations for this soup. You can substitute white wine for some of the stock (or all of it, if you're in the mood). You can cook chunked potatoes or other vegetables in the stock (peas, carrots, etc.) before adding the fish. Use your imagination and you'll wow your guests with a true and exquisite specialty of the house.

NEW ENGLAND CLAM CHOWDER

In all our samplings of soups we have never been able to surpass the New England clam chowder served at Donkins Restaurant in Marina del Rey, California. It's almost too simple to believe but, as they say, tasting is believing. With the permission of the proprietor, here it is.

5 cups chicken stock
5 cups clam juice
1 pound potatoes, peeled and diced
1 pound onions, diced
1 pound celery, diced
1 pound clams, diced
1 pint heavy cream
salt and pepper to taste

Bring combination stock and clam juice to boil and add all ingredients except cream. Simmer, covered, until the potatoes are done. Heat cream and swirl into chowder. Garnish with fresh parsley sprigs.

MANHATTAN CLAM CHOWDER

Use the same basic recipe, but omit the cream and add 2 cups diced carrots and 1 pound fresh tomatoes, peeled and pureed in the blender.

CREAM OF FISH SOUP

2 pounds uncooked shellfish or any fresh fillet of fish
5 cups fish stock
5 tablespoons butter
1 onion, chopped
1 carrot, chopped
1 large leek (white part only), chopped
1 celery stalk, chopped
bouquet garni
3 tablespoons flour
salt and pepper to taste
½ cup heavy cream
juice of ½ lemon
2 tablespoons fresh dill, finely chopped

Melt 3 tablespoons of the butter in a heavy saucepan and saute onion, carrots, leeks and celery until onion is transparent. Bring stock to boil and add fish, garni and sauteed vegetables. Simmer for about 15 minutes or until fish is done. Remove garni, pour into blender and puree. Melt remaining butter in saucepan, add flour and stir-fry until paste forms. Slowly add mixture from blender, stirring constantly. Reheat, add salt, pepper, cream, lemon juice and dill and serve garnished with grated carrots and/or tiny cooked shrimp.

CREAM OF SCALLOPS SOUP

3 cups water or mixture of 1½ cups chicken stock and
1½ cups fish stock or clam juice
1½ pounds fresh scallops
1 onion, chopped
1 carrot, chopped
5 tablespoons butter
2 cups dry white wine
bouquet garni with 7 peppercorns added
4 tablespoons flour
3 egg yolks
1 cup heavy cream
1½ cups milk
salt and pepper to taste

In a heavy saucepan, melt 2 tablespoons of the butter and stir-fry onions and carrot until onions are transparent. Puree in blender. Heat water or stock mixture along with the wine and slowly stir in onion puree. Add bouquet garni, bring to boil and simmer for 20 minutes. Dice scallops and mix into boiling pot. Cook 3 minutes (no more). Remove scallops with slotted spoon and reserve. Melt remaining butter in a heavy saucepan and stir in flour until thick paste forms. Remove garni and add paste to soup, stirring constantly. In a separate bowl, mix eggs and cream with a fork. Add a little of the hot soup to the mixture then mix into pot. Add milk, scallops, salt and pepper and stir-cook about 1 minute. Serve garnished with grated carrots or salted croutons.

• **NOTES** •

ITALIAN FISH SOUP

3 pounds any fish in season, whole
2½ quarts water
bouquet garni
1 onion, chopped
1 celery stalk, chopped
2 tablespoons olive oil
1 clove garlic, minced
2 tablespoons tomato sauce
1 pound linguine, broken
1 teaspoon anchovy paste
2 tablespoons parsley

Wash whole fish and place in pot with water, garni, onions and celery and simmer about 30 minutes. Remove fish, skin and bone it and cut into serving pieces. In heavy skillet, heat oil, add garlic and stir-fry, about 3 minutes. Add tomato sauce and cook an additional 3 minutes. Add about 4 cups of the water the fish was cooked in and bring to boil. Add linguine and simmer until cooked (about 10 minutes). Stir in anchovy paste and parsley and serve over pieces of fish placed in individual bowls.

OYSTER SOUP

3 cups chicken stock
3 cups water
3 cups clam juice
2 pints shucked oysters
4 tablespoons butter
3 tablespoons flour

2 tablespoons onion, finely chopped
½ cup celery, finely chopped
3 cups milk, scalded
1 teaspoon combination nutmeg and ground mace
3 egg yolks

Heat combined water, stock and clam juice. Wash and dice oysters. Add them to stock and simmer for 25 minutes. Melt 2 tablespoons of butter and saute celery and onion until onion is transparent. Add remaining butter, flour, milk, nutmeg and mace and stir into soup. Beat egg yolks, add about 1 tablespoon of the soup, mix well and whisk into soup. Serve garnished with salted croutons and fresh sprigs of parsley.

Variation

Substitute 3 cups canned cream-style corn for the cream.

QUICK OYSTER-CORN CHOWDER

1 pint fresh oysters
1½ cups chicken stock
1 onion, chopped
1 carrot, chopped
1 celery stalk, chopped
1½ cups water
1 pound potatoes, peeled and diced
2 tablespoons parsley
1 can cream-style corn
2 cups milk
salt and pepper to taste

Melt butter in large, heavy saucepan and sautee onions, carrots and celery until onions are transparent. Add stock, water, potatoes, parsley and cook for about 15 minutes. Add corn, cook for an additional 5 minutes; add oysters and milk and cook until oyster edges curl. Salt and pepper to taste and serve garnished with grated carrots or plain croutons.

MEXICAN FISH SOUP

10 cups fish stock
2 pounds raw halibut or cod, boned and chunked
1 onion, chopped
1 celery stalk, chopped
2 tablespoons butter
2 tablespoons flour
3 tomatoes, peeled and chopped
salt and pepper to taste

In a heavy saucepan, melt butter and saute onions and celery until onions are transparent. Sprinkle flour over mixture and stir-fry until paste forms. Heat stock, stir in paste, add fish and tomatoes, cover and simmer for about 25 minutes or until fish is done. Season to taste and serve garnished with fresh parsley leaves.

RICH-MAN'S CRAB BISQUE

3 pounds king crab meat
5 pounds crab claws, cracked
8 cups water
2 cups chicken stock
bouquet garni
5 tablespoons butter
1 onion, chopped
1 carrot, chopped
1 celery stalk, chopped
4 tablespoons flour
1 cup heavy cream
juice from ½ lemon
salt and pepper to taste

Heat water-stock mixture in heavy pot with garni. Add crab claws and simmer, covered for 1½ hours. While stock is brewing, melt butter in heavy saucepan and saute onion, carrot and celery until onion is transparent. Place in blender and puree. Put back in pan, heat and sprinkle over flour to make paste, stirring constantly. Stir in a little of the stock. Remove garni and claws from stock and slowly stir all of liquid into saucepan with the onion-carrot-celery paste. Add crab meat to soup and cook very slowly over low heat, covered. Remove meat from claws and add to soup. Heat cream and stir into mixture. Add lemon juice and seasonings and serve garnished with dollar bills.

VARIATIONS

Without seeming repetitious, you can always substitute shrimp or lobster. If you do, use 5 cups fish stock and 5 cups chicken stock.

ROMAN STYLE FISH SOUP

8 Little Neck clams, with juice
4 oysters, cut into pieces, with juice
½ cup olive oil
1 clove garlic
1 tablespoon chopped parsley
4 anchovy filets, cut into pieces
3 seeds hot pepper or 1 pinch cayenne pepper
1 cup dry red wine
1 cup canned tomatoes
½ pound halibut, cut into pieces
½ pound filet of sole, cut into pieces
½ teaspoon salt
4 slices French bread, toasted

Place clams and oysters in pan and heat until shells open. Cut oysters into pieces and strain juice of oysters and clams, reserving juice. Place olive oil and garlic in large kettle, add parsley, anchovies and pepper and brown slowly, stirring well. Add wine and cook until it evaporates. Add tomatoes and cook 5 minutes. Add all the fish, clams, oysters, oyster and clam juice. Add salt and enough water to cover fish and cook 30 minutes, adding more water is necessary, as soup should not be too condensed. Place a slice of toasted bread in each dish and pour soup over it.

MUSSEL SOUP

9 pounds mussels
9 shallots
6 sprigs parsley
4½ cups dry white wine
6 small onions, quartered
6 tablespoons butter

2 bay leaves
1½ teaspoon thyme
salt, freshly ground white pepper
cayenne
3 egg yolks, lightly beaten
6 cups heavy cream

Scrub mussels and pull out beards. Put in pot with shallots, parsley, wine, onions, butter and herbs. Bring to boil, then reduce heat and simmer for 5 minutes, until shells open. Strain liquid into large heavy pan. Just before serving, blend cream and egg yolks. Stir in a little of the hot soup, then pour into soup. Stir over low heat until slightly thickened.

SHELLFISH-BUTTERMILK BISQUE

(GOOD HOT OR COLD)

2 pounds lobster, shrimp or crab (or combination of all)
2 cups clam juice
2 cups chicken stock
2 onions, chopped
1 carrot, grated
2 tablespoons parsley, minced
3 tablespoons butter
2 cucumbers, peeled and diced
6 cups buttermilk
1 tablespoon fresh lemon juice
salt and pepper to taste

Melt butter in heavy saucepan and stir-fry onions, carrot and parsley until onion is transparent. Add cucumbers, cook an additional 3 minutes. Chop seafood coarsely, reserving some for garnish in each dish. Put stock and clam juice in blender, add onions, carrots, parsley and cucumber and puree. Pour into large pot and slowly stir in buttermilk, lemon juice and salt and pepper. Heat, but do not boil, if you're serving it hot. To serve cold, chill for at least 3 hours.

SHELLFISH GAZPACHO

2 pounds mixture of lobster, crab and shrimp
½ cup fresh lemon juice
6 cups fresh tomato juice
1 garlic clove, pressed
3 eggs, hard-boiled
1 teaspoon Dijon mustard
1 cucumber, diced
1 red onion, diced
1 green bell pepper, diced
3 tomatoes, diced
⅛ cup vegetable oil
pinch each of chili powder, salt, pepper,
Tabasco and Worcestershire sauce

Place lemon juice, 3 cups of the tomato juice, garlic, egg yolks and mustard in blender and liquefy. Then stir in rest of ingredients. Chill and serve in chilled bowls. Have extra bowls of diced tomatoes, cucumber, onion, bell pepper, hard-boiled egg whites and croutons to pass around.

SHELLFISH SOUP ROYALE

2 cups lobster, shrimp or crab
4 cups chicken stock
1½ cups clam juice
1 onion, chopped
1 carrot, chopped
1 celery stalk, chopped
5 tablespoons butter
3 tablespoons flour
2 egg yolks
1 cup heavy cream
bouquet garni

In heavy saucepan, melt 3 tablespoons butter and gently saute the vegetables (until onion is transparent). Place in blender and puree. Put back in saucepan, melt additional butter in the mixture, stirring constantly, and sprinkle over flour. Stir-fry until thickened. Stir in mixture of stock and clam juice. Add garni and simmer for about 30 minutes. If fish is uncooked, add and simmer an additional 10 minutes. If fish is already cooked, wait until after adding beaten egg yolks and cream.

•   **NOTES**   •

SHRIMP GUMBO

2½ pounds cooked shrimp
2½ cups fish stock
3 cups chicken stock
5 bacon strips
¾ cups green onions, chopped
1 clove garlic, minced
5 tablespoons flour
1 pound fresh tomatoes, peeled and chunked
2 cups cooked ham, diced
bouquet garni
1 pound fresh okra, peeled and chopped
salt and pepper to taste
1½ cup cooked rice

Fry bacon in large, heavy pan. Remove, cool and crumble. Saute onions and garlic in bacon grease, sprinkle on the flour and stir-fry until thickened. Combine stocks and slowly stir into bacon grease-flour mixture. Add tomatoes, ham and bouquet garni, cover and simmer for about 35 minutes. Add okra and cook an additional 15 minutes. Remove garni, add shrimp and simmer for about 3 minutes or until shrimp is hot. Mix in rice and serve garnished with bacon bits.

VARIATIONS

As is the case with almost any shellfish recipe, you can mix or match crabmeat, lobster or shrimp.

TROUT CHOWDER

2 cups chicken stock
3 cups water
4 pounds fresh trout
bouquet garni
1 carrot, chopped
1 onion, chopped
1 celery stalk, chopped
2 potatoes, peeled and cubed
4 tablespoons butter
1 pint heavy cream
salt and pepper to taste

Bring stock-water combination to boil. Add garni and fish. Simmer until trout is done (about 10 minutes or when it flakes). Remove and set aside. Add carrots, onion and celery and simmer about 5 more minutes. Add potatoes and cook until they are tender. Remove all bones from fish and put back into soup. Remove garni, swirl in butter and cream and serve garnished with grated carrots or salted croutons.

TUNA FISH CHOWDER

1 pound canned tuna in vegetable oil
2 cups water
2 cups chicken stock
2 strips bacon
1 onion, chopped
2 carrots, diced
2 potatoes, peeled and cubed
1 celery stalk, chopped
bouquet garni

Fry bacon in heavy saucepan and remove. Add onion, celery and carrots and stir-fry until onions are transparent. Add water and stock, garni and potatoes and simmer about 30 minutes. Flake tuna and stir into soup along with its oil. Heat and serve garnished with fresh parsley sprigs.

nine

EXOTICS FROM
'ROUND THE WORLD

Irish humorist Brian Nolen (we know some would argue that all Irishmen are humorists or at least humorous, but never mind) called his home "The Past" and had a sign over the front door proclaiming that fact. This was so everyone would know where he dwelt, you see. Well, it's also where almost all recipes originated (in the past, not in The Past). As Perla Meyers once pointed out, there are no new recipes, just minor or major changes in old ones. And when you get into recipes of other nations, they can be very old indeed . . . and very different.

Chinese, Australian, Indonesian (and so on and so on) dishes are, in our eyes, exotic. Of course, they are not exotic to the natives of China, Australia, Indonesian (and so on and so on). To them, they are perfectly normal, even mundane. There is a simple reason for this: the dishes of all nations are based on the dominant foods of those nations. While we in the United States could spend weeks, even months, trying to acquire *boembo godok*, your average Indonesian simply steps outside his door, picks a few herbs and mixes them up. Conversely, your average Indonesian would have great difficulty running down even a single tortilla in his land. This is particularly true with oils. Italian cookbooks always list olive oil as an ingredient in dishes. Why? Because olive oil is the dominant oil in Italy and, therefore, the cheapest (they would pay a premium for Wesson oil). In the Mideast, apricot oil is the dominant oil, so naturally many Mideast recipes call for its inclusion. What we're trying to point out is that one man's hamburger is another's *kamaboko*.

Now, with that clear, let's get along with the business at hand—of sharing with you some dishes from other lands. We have, however, cleverly moved them from the exotic to the exoteric (there's one for you crossword fans) so that you won't be scurrying from one gourmet shop to another looking for ingredients.

BASIC JAPANESE STOCK (DASHI)

3 quarts water
4 inch square of dried kelp (kombu)
1½ cups flaked dried bonito (katsoubushi)

Bring water to boil and add kelp. When water comes back to boil, immediately remove the kelp. Add bonito and stir. Remove from heat and allow to cool for about 10 minutes. Pour stock through cheesecloth. This stock is used by the Japanese for all their soups and as a base for stews. They also use it to cook vegetables.

FILIPINO GINGER-CHICKEN SOUP

5 cups chicken stock
5 cups water
3 pounds chicken pieces
4 tablespoons oil
2 teaspoons fresh ginger root, finely chopped
2 onions, chopped
1 cup fresh spinach leaves

Heat oil in heavy saucepan and add ginger. Stir-fry for about a minute. Add onions and saute until onions are transparent. With a slotted spoon, remove onions and ginger. Add chicken and brown well on all sides. Add chicken stock-water mixture, onions and ginger and simmer for about one hour or until chicken is done. Stir in spinach leaves and salt and pepper to taste and serve immediately.

VIETNAMESE CRAB-ASPARAGUS SOUP

8 cups chicken stock
6 dried Chinese mushrooms
1 onion, chopped
1½ pounds crab meat
2 pounds asparagus, cut into 1 inch pieces
2 teaspoons scallions, chopped
2 teaspoons cornstarch (or 1 teaspoon arrowroot)
2 eggs

Cover the mushrooms with about a cup of warm water and let them soak for 30 minutes. Drain and save water. Remove caps and thinly slice mushrooms. Heat stock and add onions and mushroom water. Simmer about 10 minutes. Add crab meat, asparagus and scallions and simmer until asparagus is cooked (about 10 minutes). Combine cornstarch with a little cold water and stir into soup, stirring constantly until soup thickens. Beat eggs well and dribble into soup slowly to form egg ribbons.

SOUTH AFRICAN BUTTERMILK SOUP (KALTSCHALE)

2 quarts buttermilk
6 slices pumpernickel bread, toasted
¾ cup seedless raisins
4 tablespoons confectioner's sugar
2½ teaspoons lemon rind, finely grated
1 teaspoon cinnamon
1 teaspoon nutmeg

Pulverize toast in blender. Place in bowl and add raisins (soak them first for about 10 minutes in warm milk and drain), sugar, lemon rind, cinnamon and nutmeg. Mix well and slowly stir in the buttermilk. Chill for at least 1 hour before serving, garnish with additional cinnamon and nutmeg and thin slices of cucumber.

EAST AFRICAN AVOCADO-TOMATO SOUP

1 pound tomatoes, peeled and pureed
2 avocados, pureed
1 cup sour cream
½ cup milk
3 tablespoons fresh lemon juice
1 tablespoon vegetable oil
salt and pepper to taste

Mix all ingredients in large bowl. Chill and serve garnished with thin slices of cucumber.

RUSSIAN YOGURT-BARLEY SOUP

2 quarts water
¼ cup uncooked barley
2 cups plain yogurt
4 eggs
2 tablespoons flour
2 tablespoons butter
2 teaspoons coriander, finely chopped
2 tablespoons onion, finely chopped

Heat one quart of the water and simmer barley in it until done (about 45 minutes). Drain and reserve barley. In a large bowl, pour in remaining quart of water and slowly add yogurt, stirring until dissolved. Pour into heavy saucepan and bring to simmer. In separate bowl, beat eggs and slowly stir in the flour. Stir into yogurt-water mixture and continue heating, being careful not to boil. Stir in barley, onions, butter and coriander and heat for about 3 minutes longer. Serve garnished with fresh parsley sprigs or mint leaves.

TURKISH YOGURT-CUCUMBER SOUP

4 cups plain yogurt
1 large cucumber, peeled, seeded and pureed
3 teaspoons white vinegar
1 teaspoon oil
⅓ teaspoon fresh dill, chopped

Place yogurt in large bowl and mix until smooth. Gently add remaining ingredients, stir well and chill. Serve garnished with fresh mint leaves or thin cucumber slices.

GREEK EGG AND LEMON SOUP

8 cups chicken stock
½ cup uncooked rice
5 eggs
3 tablespoons fresh lemon juice
salt and pepper to taste

Bring stock to boil and add rice. Simmer until almost cooked (about 15 minutes). In separate bowl, beat eggs well (until frothy). Add lemon juice and about ½ cup of the heated stock. Swirl into stock and continue cooking about 5 minutes (until soup thickens). Serve garnished with fresh mint leaves.

ISRAELI FRUIT SOUP (MARAK PEROT KAR)

6 cups water
1 cantaloupe, diced
1 quart strawberries
½ pound seedless grapes
3 apples, peeled and diced
¾ cup fresh lemon juice
½ cup sugar or ⅓ cup honey
1½ cups fresh orange juice

Bring water to boil and add all fruits and sugar or honey. Simmer 20 minutes and remove from heat. Stir in lemon juice and allow to cool. Puree in blender, add orange juice and chill for at least 1 hour before serving. Garnish with fresh mint leaves, sour cream or whipped cream.

MANGO BISQUE

3 mangos
2 cups unsweetened pineapple juice
1 tablespoon fresh lemon juice
1 jigger dark rum
½ teaspoon nutmeg

Blend all ingredients in blender until smooth, chill and serve garnished with thin slices of cucumber.

SHARON CADWALLADER'S MEXICAN SQUASH BLOOM SOUP (SOPA DE FLOR DE CALABAZA)

1 pound summer squash blossoms (or pumpkin blossoms)
1 onion, chopped fine
8 tablespoons butter
1½ quarts milk
2 tablespoons flour
2 egg yolks
½ cup cream
1 cup bread cubes
salt and pepper to taste

Remove stems and chop blossoms. With onion, saute in 2 tablespoons of the butter. Cover and simmer until tender. Blend onions with 1 cup milk in blender. Melt 4 tablespoons butter, add flour and stir until smooth. Add to blender ingredients to make thick sauce. Add this mixture to remaining milk heating in soup pot. Season to taste and remove from heat when slightly thickened. Beat egg yolks and cream together. Fry bread cubes in remaining butter and add with yolks and cream to hot, but not boiling, soup. Serve with lime or lemon wedges and a hot pepper.

POLYNESIAN AVOCADO-MACADAMIA NUT SOUP

3 avocados
1½ cups macadamia nuts, chopped
2 cups chicken stock
1 tablespoon fresh lemon juice
1 clove garlic
2 cups heavy cream

Reserving ½ cup nuts, place all ingredients in blender and blend until smooth. Chill and serve garnished with the reserved nuts and parsley sprigs.

SHERRY BOUILLON

4 cups beef stock
4 cups dry sherry

Combine and simmer for 1 hour. Serve either hot or cold, garnished with thin slices of fresh lime.

SHERRY-CRAB SOUP

6 cups chicken stock
1 pound crab meat
1½ cups dry sherry
1 tablespoon fresh lemon juice
2 teaspoons grated lemon peel
1 tablespoon onion, finely grated
1 cup heavy cream

Marinate crab in wine for 1 hour. Heat stock and add lemon juice, peel, onion, salt and pepper to taste, and crab-wine mixture. Stir in cream and serve garnished with fresh parsley sprigs or mint leaves. This soup is good hot or cold.

SOUPE DU JURADE

4 cups cream of tomato soup
1 onion, chopped
1 garlic clove, minced
1 tablespoon oil
2 tablespoons butter
bouquet garni
1 egg yolk
4 tablespoons heavy cream
4 tablespoons grated Swiss cheese

Brown onion and garlic in oil-butter mixture and then pour over the soup. Add garni and simmer, but do not boil, for about 30 minutes. Remove garni, mix yolk and cream, pour on top and serve hot, garnished with cheese.

SENEGALESE

3 cups chicken stock
2 cups heavy cream
2 teaspoons curry powder
1 cup cracked ice

Blend stock, curry and 1 cup of the cream until smooth. Add remaining cream and ice to blender and blend at high speed for about 10 seconds. Serve immediately, garnished with fresh parsley sprigs, additional curry or thin cucumber slices.

ECUADORIAN RAW SHRIMP SOUP

1 pound shrimp, peeled and deveined
juice of 5 limes
juice of 2 lemons
rinds of lemons, grated
2 onions, sliced very thin
1 cup tomato juice
½ cup dry white wine
2 tablespoons oil
2 tablespoons catsup
1 teaspoon Worcestershire sauce
1 dash Tabasco
1 garlic clove, crushed
2 tomatoes, peeled and diced
1 avocado, diced
¼ cup stuffed olives
¼ cup chopped parsley

Marinate shrimp for at least 6 hours in combined lemon and lime juices. In pan, heat tomato juice and wine and boil onions for 2 minutes. Remove and cool. When cool, pour over shrimp. Add lemon rind, oil, catsup, Worcestershire, Tabasco and garlic. Stir and serve cold, garnished with tomatoes, avocado, olives and parsley. NOTE: The marinate "cooks" the shrimp, so don't worry about it being as raw as the recipe might imply.

FRENCH MUSTARD SOUP

5 cups chicken stock
2½ cups milk
3 tablespoons butter
3 tablespoons flour
salt and pepper to taste
3 teaspoons onion juice
4 egg yolks
6 tablespoons Dijon mustard

Melt butter in heavy saucepan and sprinkle over the flour. Stir-fry until paste is formed. Stir in stock and then milk. Add salt, pepper and onion juice and simmer, but do not boil, for about 5 minutes. In separate bowl, mix yolks, cream and mustard with ½ cup of the hot stock. Swirl into soup and serve hot, garnished with garlic croutons and fresh parsley sprigs.

MOROCCAN LAMB SOUP (HARIRA)

5 cups chicken stock
5 cups lamb stock
2 pounds lamb meat, diced
1 onion, chopped
⅓ cup garbanzo beans
⅓ teaspoon ground ginger
¼ teaspoon powdered saffron
¼ teaspoon paprika
3 tablespoons butter
3 cups cooked rice
1 tablespoon dried yeast
4 tomatoes, peeled and pureed
5 tablespoons fresh parsley, chopped
salt and pepper to taste

Bring stock mixture to boil and add lamb, onions, garbanzo beans, ginger, saffron, paprika and butter. Simmer until lamb is done (about 1½ hours). Add rice and continue simmering over low heat. Dilute the yeast in a little water, place in saucepan with tomato puree and parsley and simmer for about 15 minutes. Mix into soup and serve garnished with more parsley or mint leaves.

COCONUT-FISH-CORNED BEEF SOUP

8 cups chicken stock
2 onions, chopped
2 celery stalks, chopped
2 carrots, chopped
1 green pepper, seeded and diced
4 pounds fresh fish, boned
1 pound corned beef
4 tablespoons corn meal
1 pound grated coconut

Bring stock to boil and add vegetables. Simmer about 30 minutes and add fish. Simmer until fish is done. Remove fish and set aside. Chunk corned beef and add to stock. Simmer until done. Swirl in the corn meal and coconut and simmer 10 minutes. Add fish to stock and simmer until fish is heated. Serve with corn meal mush wedges.

BUCKINGHAM PALACE SOUP

This soup is purported to have been Queen Victoria's favorite.

10 cups chicken stock
1 onion, chopped
1 celery stalk, chopped
2 tablespoons butter
2 tablespoons flour
bouquet garni
½ cup cracker crumbs
2 cups cooked chicken, diced
1 tablespoon fresh sage, chopped
2 cups light cream
salt and pepper to taste
3 eggs, hard-boiled and chopped fine

Melt butter in heavy saucepan and stir-fry onions and celery until onions are transparent. Sprinkle over the flour and stir-fry until paste is formed. Slowly stir in the stock, add garni and simmer, covered, for 30 minutes. Remove garni. Mix in the cracker crumbs, chicken, sage, salt, pepper and eggs and simmer an additional 3 minutes. Swirl in heated light cream. Serve garnished with fresh parsley sprigs.

MANDARIN ORANGE SOUP

5 cups beef stock
½ pound tomatoes, skinned and pureed
1 onion, chopped
3 small cans mandarin oranges
1 tablespoon honey

Puree tomatoes, onion, honey and oranges (reserve some for garnish) in blender. Heat stock and swirl in vegetable-fruit puree. Remove from heat, chill and serve cold, garnished with fresh parsley sprigs and orange sections.

IRISH STEW SOUP

3 tablespoons butter
2 onions, sliced
2 carrots, chunked
4 cups cabbage, shredded
3 tablespoons flour
5 cups water
5 cups beef stock
3 pounds stewing beef
bouquet garni
1 cup fresh peas
1 cup barley
1 potato per person
2 turnips, chunked

Melt butter in heavy saucepan and stir-fry onions, carrots and cabbage until onions are transparent. Sprinkle over flour and stir until paste is formed. Slowly add stock-water mixture, meat and garni. Simmer 1 hour. Add peas, barley, potatoes and turnips and simmer an additional hour. Add cabbage and simmer an additional 15 minutes. Remove garni and potatoes. Place 1 potato in each bowl and pour soup over it.

FINNISH HOLIDAY SOUP

5 cups water
5 cups beef stock
2 pounds beef ribs, broken
3 cups yellow peas
7 whole allspice
1 onion, chopped
1 celery stalk, chopped
bouquet garni

Heat stock-water mixture and add all ingredients. Simmer for at least 4 hours, remove garni and serve garnished with croutons.

• NOTES •

AFTERWORD

Dorothy Parker, America's great acid-tongued lady of letters, had a special fondness of animals and somehow one evening came into possession of two baby alligators. The next day she was due at work bright and early so she left them in the bathtub, figuring she would find a proper home for them sometime during the day. When she returned in the evening, she found this note from her maid:

"I won't be back. I don't work in places where they have alligators. I would have told you this before, but I never thought the subject would come up."

Well, we didn't tell you something in the beginning of this book because, had the subject come up, many of you would have read no further. That is that we are basically "health-fooders," to use a term we don't really like. That's why, in most instances anyway, we have given you honey as a substitute for sugar and arrowroot as a substitute for cornstarch. Both are better and better for you. We should probably also provide you with our definition of health foods. They are, simply, foods grown without chemical assistance and containing all of the nutrients nature intended for them to have. They are foods rich in natural vitamins and minerals, protein, carbohydrates and natural sugars. Essentially, so-called health foods are the foods the way they were at the turn of the century, grown naturally and presented in their own packages, not in cardboard, plastic or tin.

When we started this project, we had all intentions of providing you with what the title implies—the *ultimate* soup cookbook and that meant to us a complete listing of all soups known to man. It was a grandiose plan to say the least. We immediately discovered three things: (1) that if you took all the soup recipes from around the world, they would fill an encyclopedia, (2) that testing them all would take five years and severely strain our pocketbooks, our minds and our marriage, and (3) that the differences are mainly local flavorings of things fresh and available there. In Chinese cookery alone we compiled more than 75 different recipes only to put them back in our files. Where—if you lived in Eau Claire, Wisconsin, or Billings, Montana, for instance—would you find fresh black fungus, bean-thread noodles, serehpoeder, boemboe Godok or dried forest needles? Even if you could locate them the quality would probably be questionable. The same problem presents itself when you get into Mideast and even some European dishes. So, realizing that there are places in the United States where you still can't find something even as familiar as tortillas, we took a different course. We have included only recipes that contain easily available ingredients. That's why you won't find a turtle soup in this book. It is illegal to import them.

As we said in the Foreword, we tested all the recipes. We hope you, in time, will do so, too, and that you will enjoy them as much as we and our friends have.

INDEX